Eostre
Ostara   Eostar

Facts, assumptions, conjectures,
speculations, guesses
and nonsense

GardenStone

Copyright: GardenStone, 2015
E-Mail: GardenStone@boudicca.de
Internet: www.boudicca.de
Internet: www.facebook.com/GardenStone

Editing and proofreading: Lisa Star
Design, cover and layout: GardenStone

All rights reserved; no part of this publication may be reproduced or transmitted by any means, electronic, mechanical, photocopying or otherwise, without the prior written permission of the copyrightholder.

Printing and publishing:
BoD - Books on Demand, Norderstedt, Germany
ISBN 978-3-7386-5577-3

Contents

Preface 3

Standard sources and etymology 7
   The Venerable Bede and Eostre 7
   The Anglo-Saxon Penitentials 14
   Jacob Grimm and Ostara 19
   Saxon transfer 22
   Charlemagne and April 25
   The Austriahena goddesses 29

Some possible etymology 33

Ostara, Ostera, Osta and Eostar on the continent 39
   The Goddess Hurstrga 39
   The Osta-Stone 40
   Ostara at Osterholz 42
   Oostera – Oostera festival 44
   De Ostera Saxonum 46
   Ostara and Osterode 48
   The Sandstone rock formation "Externsteine" 51
   Ostera at the Ohlenborg castle 53
   The Zedler Lexicon 55
   Münchhausen's "Wold and Ostar" 57
   Political accommodation 60
   The Blankenburg Oster-Stone 60
   The Corvey 'Eostar' field blessing 62
   The Gambach 'Oistirsteynen' 70
   Forms of Easter in names of places and people 72

Tradition and folklore.. 77
    Easter Bunny, Easter eggs 78
    Easter bonfires 81
    More Lore, Customs and Traditions 86

Afterword – Some Final Remarks 95

Gratitude is expressed to 99

Used sources 101
    Illustrations 101
    Literature..103
    Webpages..106

Index..108

Preface

In this book, the author does not declare himself against or in favor of the existence of a goddess Ostara, Eostre or Eostar; that would be mainly a religious position. A religious view concerning such a goddess does not necessarily need the information provided here.

Only the results of historical, mythological, folkloric, literary and linguistic research concerning Eostre / Ostara / Eostar (written that way or in some other spelling) are presented here.

About Eostre and Ostara quite an amount of research exists. In books, articles or web pages a lot can be found about these deity names. The alert seeker will soon notice, that for very many authors, most of the information they provide has been copied from other contemporary "colleagues". Especially on the web this has become almost a habit unfortunately.

This treatise is yet another text about Eostre and Ostara. In fact, there is more provided about Ostara, the continental counterpart of Eostre, simply because of the greater number of sources found.

Sources of diverse quality were used, some of them quite heavily disputed concerning their reliability or validity. That is an important reason not to take all the information presented here for correct, true or valid. Related to that is the customary tendency to accept as self-evident information cited from known or famous sources as reliable and trustworthy – that is not an advisable habit!

Similar is the general trusting attitude towards famous authors. Yet, because Bede, Grimm, Einhard, etc. wrote this and that, it does not automatically mean they are right. In almost all cases, their sources or intentions can not be checked anymore and their deductions often can not stand up to modern methods of research and science. The current validity of the related works of almost all of them is meanwhile repeatedly discussed in scholarly depth by quite a few authors. In their time, these men undoubtedly were excellent scholars, but in the course of time, due to development in many fields of science, scientific standards have changed. What Bede or Grimm may have seen as reliable sources do not stand as such today. Many are seen as obscure at best. Additionally, what they may have considered high standards of scientific research and methodology are one or the other currently not accepted as valid science at all.

Therefore, those "old hats" should be taken critically and with restraint and so this work has to be taken in hand. Related to that, please reread the subtitle above and try yourself to sort the variety of pieces of information provided here into the appropriate categories; that may encourage critical thinking.

Recent sources which, according to the opinion of the author clearly belong to New Age, esoteric, religious practice and fantasy categories, have been studiously avoided.

During the research the oldest found source for a deity

"Ostara" dates from the 16th century. That does not mean she is not mentioned in earlier sources. It just means, no such sources were found within the time set for this small project. Unfortunately without more detailed information, in several sources from the 16th and 17th centuries it is referred to old records from the 12th and 13th centuries in which an Ostera is mentioned who is told to be honored. And although in a document from 1147 the 'Mark Ostera' (a countship) near Paderborn in Germany is mentioned, a connection with a goddess Ostera is not recorded in that document.

Quite a few citations from old German books were added. Please do not think the authors wrote those works in English, rather those citations were translated for the English edition of this work.

And, in a finishing remark of this foreword, the author has to admit that at several places in the text he has made it easy for himself. Where it concerned topics he already wrote something about in one of his other publications, he simply pasted those pieces of text here, instead of writing the same again in other words.

GardenStone,
Usingen Summer/Autumn 2015.

Eostre – Ostara: "The Dawn Bringer" by Pollyanna Jones

Standard sources and etymology

The Venerable Bede and Eostre

Almost always when the goddess Eostre is a topic of discussion, it starts with the "Bede-reference". That is not really a surprise, because the name of the goddess Eostre was recorded for the first time by the English monk, historian and author Bede, 672/673-735, (Beda Venerabilis, the Venerable Bede, Saint Bede). In the 8th Century he published his Latin work "DE TEMPORUM RATIONE" (The Reckoning of Time), and in chapter 15 of that work it reads about this goddess:

> **In olden time the English people -- for it did not seem fitting to me that I should speak of other people's observance of the year and yet be silent about my own nation's -- calculated their months according to the course of the moon. Hence, after the manner of the Greeks and the Romans (the months) take their name from the Moon, for the Moon is called mona and the month monath.**
>
> **The first month, which the Latins call January, is Giuli; February is called Solmonath; March Hrethmonath; April, Eosturmonath; May, Thrimilchi; June, Litha; July, also Litha; August, Weodmonath; September, Halegmonath; October, Winterfilleth; November, Blodmonath; December, Giuli, the same name by which January is called.**

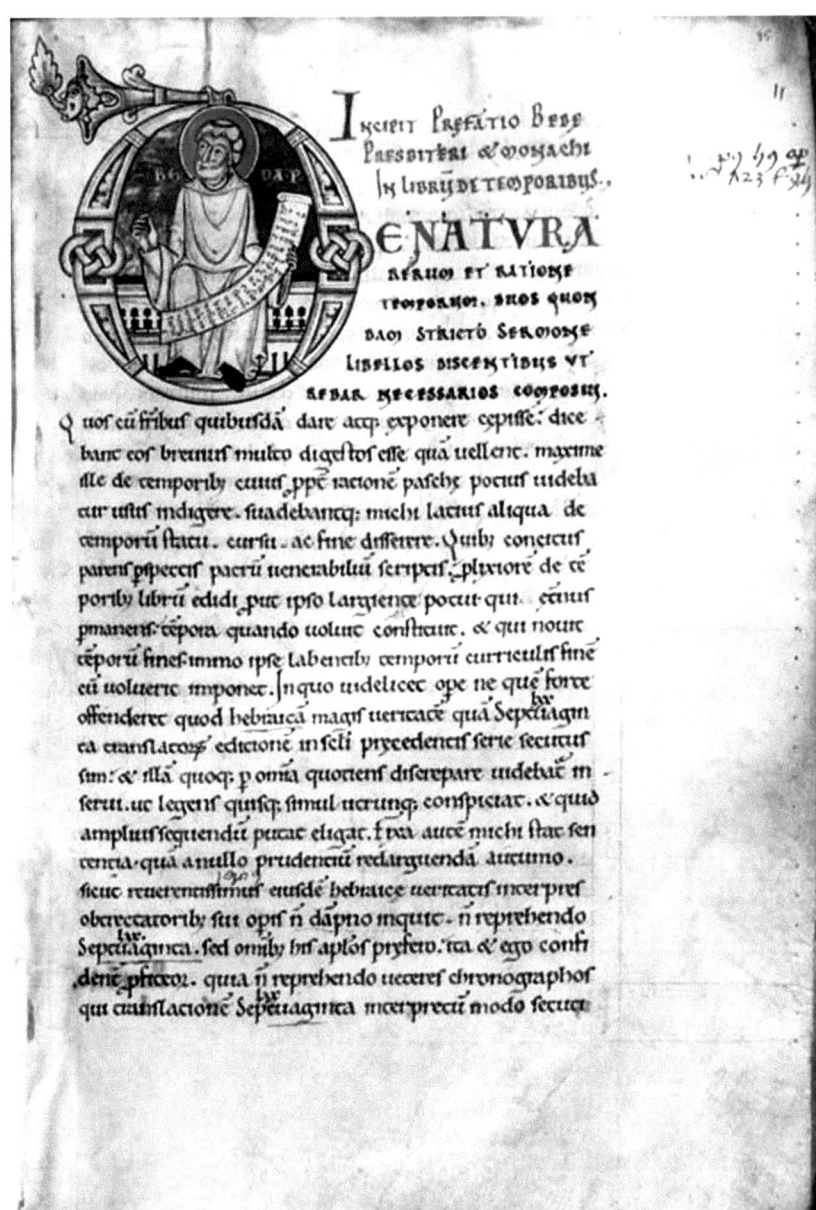

"De temporum Ratione", startpage

They began the year on the 8th kalends of January (25 December), when we celebrate the birth of the Lord. That very night, which we hold so sacred, they used to call by the heathen word Modranecht, that is, "mothers' night", because (we suspect) of the ceremonies they enacted all that night.

Whenever it was a common year, they gave three lunar months to each season. When an embolismic* year occurred (that is, one of 13 lunar months) they assigned the extra month to summer, so that three months together bore the name "Litha"; hence they called (the embolismic) year "Thrilithi". It had four summer months, with the usual three for the other seasons. But originally, they divided the year as a whole into two seasons, summer and winter, assigning the six months in which the days are longer than the nights to summer, and the other six to winter. Hence they called the month in which the winter season began "Winterfilleth", a name made up from "winter" and "full moon", because winter began on the full moon of that month.

Nor is it irrelevant if we take the time to translate the names of the other months. The months of Giuli derive their name from the day when the sun turns back (and begins) to increase, because one of (these months) precedes (this day) and the other follows.

Solmonath can be called "month of cakes",

which they offered to their gods in that month.

Hrethmonath is named for their goddess Hretha, to whom they sacrificed at this time. Eosturmonath has a name which is now translated "Paschal month", and which was once called after a goddess of theirs named Eostre, in whose honour feasts were celebrated in that month. Now they designate that Paschal season by her name, calling the joys of the new rite by the time-honoured name of the old observance.

Thrimilchi was so called because in that month the cattle were milked three times a day; such, at one time, was the fertility of Britain or Germany, from whence the English nation came to Britain. Litha means "gentle" or "navigable", because in both these months the calm breezes are gentle, and they were wont to sail upon the smooth sea.

Weodmonath means "month of tares", for they are very plentiful then. Halegmonath means "month of sacred rites". Winterfilleth can be called by the invented composite name "winter-full". Blodmonath is "month of immolations", for their cattle which were to be slaughtered were consecrated to their gods. Good Jesu, thanks be to thee, who has turned us away from these vanities and given us (grace) to offer to thee the sacrifice of praise.

Wallis translation

* Embolismic: points to a system of timekeeping that defines the beginning and length and divisions of the year.

For those who want to check the correctness of this translation, or make their own, here is the original Latin text of the related part of Bede's chapter:

CAPUT XV:

DE MENSIBUS ANGLORUM

ANTIQUI AUTEM ANGLORUM POPULI (NEQUE ENIM MIHI CONGRUUM VIDETUR, ALIARUM GENTIUM ANNALEM OBSERVANTIAM DICERE, ET MEAE RETICERE) IUXTA CURSUM LUNAE SUOS MENSES COMPUTAVERE; UNDE ET A LUNA HEBRAEORUM ET GRAECORUM MORE NOMEN ACCIPIUNT. SI QUIDEM APUD EOS LUNA MONA, MENSIS MONATH APPELLATUR. PRIMUSQUE EORUM MENSIS, QUIDEM LATINI JANUARIUM VOCANT, DICITUR GIULI. DEINDE FEBRUARIUS SOL-MONATH, MARTIUS RHED-MONATH, APRILIS **EOSTUR- MONATH**, MAIUS THRIMYLCHI, JUNIUS LIDA, JULIUS SIMILITER LIDA, AUGUSTUS VUEOD-MONATH, SEPTEMBER HALEG-MONATH, OKTOBER VUINTERFYLLETH, NOVEMBER BLOD-MONATH, DECEMBER GIULI, EODEM JANUARIUS NOMINE VOCATUR. INCIPIEBANT AUTEM ANNUM AB OCTAVO CALENDARUM JANUARIARUM DIE, UBI NUNC NATALE DOMINI CELEBRAMUS. ET IPSAM NOCTEM NUNC NOBIS SACROSANCTUM, TUNC GENTILI VOCABULO MODRANICHT, ID EST, MATRUM NOCTEM, APPELLABANT, OB CAUSAM, UT SUSPICAMUR. CEREMONIARUM QUAS IN EA PERVIGILES AGEBANT. ET QUOTIESCUNQUE COMMUNIS ESSET ANNUS, TERNOS MENSES

LUNARES SINGULIS ANNI TEMPORIBUS DABANT. CUM VERO EMBOLISMUS, HOC EST, XIII MENSIUM LUNARIUM ANNUS OCCURRERET, SUPERFLUUM MENSEM AESTATI APPONEBANT, ITA UT TUNC TRES MENSES SIMUL LIDA NOMINE VOCARENTUR, ET OB ID ANNUS ILLE THRILIDI COGNOMINABATUR, HABENS IV MENSES AESTATIS, TERNOS UT SEMPER TEMPORUM CAETERORUM. ITEM PRINCIPALITER ANNUM TOTUM IN DUO TEMPORA, HYEMIS, VIDELICET, ET AESTATIS DISPARTIEBANT, SEX ILLOS MENSES QUIBUS LONGIORES NOCTIBUS DIES SUNT AESTATI TRIBUENDO, SEX RELIQUOS HYEMI. UNDE ET MENSEM QUO HYEMALIA TEMPORA INCIPIEBANT VUINTER-FYLLETH APPELLABANT, COMPOSITO NOMINE AB HYEME ET PLENILUNIO, QUIA VIDELICET A PLENILUNIO EIUSDEM MENSIS HYEMS SORTIRETUR INITIUM. NEC AB RE EST SI ET CAETERA MENSIUM EORUM QUID SIGNIFICENT NOMINA INTERPRETARI CUREMUS.

MENSES GIULI A CONVERSIONE SOLIS IN AUCTUM DIEI, QUIA UNUS EORUM PRAECEDIT, ALIUS SUBSEQUITUR, NOMINA ACCIPIUNT. SOL-MONATH DICI POTEST MENSIS PLACENTARUM, QUAS IN EO DIIS SUIS OFFEREBANT; RHED-MONATH A DEO ILLORUM RHEDA, CUI IN ILLO SACRIFICABANT, NOMINATUR; **EOSTUR-MONATH**, QUI NUNC PASCHALIS MENSIS INTERPRETETUR, QUONDAM **A DEA ILLORUM QUAE EOSTRE** VOCABATUR, ET CUI IN ILLO FESTA CELEBRABANT, NOMEN HABUIT, A CUIUS NOMINE NUNC PASCHALE TEMPUS COGNOMINANT; CONSUETO ANTIQUAE OBSERVATIONIS VOCABULO GAUDIA NOVAE SOLEMNITATIS VOCANTES. TRI-MILCHI DICEBATUR, QUOD TRIBUS VICIBUS IN EO PER DIEM PECORA MULGEBANTUR.

TALIS ENIM ERAT QUONDAM UBERTAS BRITANNIAE, VEL GERMANIAE, DE QUA IN BRITANNIAM NATIO INTRAVIT ANGLORUM. LIDA DICITUR BLANDUS, SIVE NAVIGABILIS, QUOD IN UTROQUE MENSE ET BLANDA SIT SERENITAS AURARUM, ET NAVIGARI SOLEANT AEQUORA. VUEOD-MONATH MENSIS ZIZANIORUM, QUOD EA TEMPESTATE MAXIME ABUNDENT. HALEGH-MONATH MENSIS SACRO-RUM. VUINTER-FYLLETH POTEST DICI COMPOSITO NOVO NOMINE HYEMEPLENILUNIUM. BLOT-MONATH MENSIS IMMOLATIONUM, QUIA IN EA PECORA QUAE OCCISURI ERANT DIIS SUIS VOVERENT. GRATIAS TIBI, BONE JESU, QUI NOS, AB HIS VANIS AVERTENS, TIBI SACRIFICIA LAU-DIS OFFERE DONASTI.

Stephen Pollington in his book The Elder Gods from 2011, at p. 226, offers a possible interesting detail concerning Bede's remark:

> "Eostur-monath has a name which is now translated "Paschal month", and which was once called after a goddess of theirs named Eostre, in whose honour feasts were celebrated in that month."

Pollington comments:

> Bede's mention of feasts held in her honour implies that a surplus of food was available for these celebrations; in spring, this would probably be dairy produce rather than ripened crops. Interestingly, Ælfric in his homily ALIUS

SERMO DE DIE PASCHAE (Another thing about Easter Day), mentions some deplorable practices associated with the week before Easter:

Forwel fela sind þe wyllað on ðisum dagum drincan oð speowðan 7 fracodlice him betwynan sacian.

Far too many there are who in these days wish to drink until they spew, and to contend wickedly among themselves.

The impression is of alcoholic celebrations to greet the spring, and perhaps high-spiritedness leading to squabbles and fights.

Stephen Pollington

The British writer and illustrator Pollyanna Jones wrote on Facebook in a laughing reply to this quote:

In all fairness, most of our fairs get pretty rowdy and raucous. Traditions die hard over here.

The Anglo-Saxon Penitentials

A series of lists of sins and the penances prescribed for them exist from Anglo-Saxon times. The oldest known ones date from the 6th Century and more were added in subsequent centuries. Among other contributors are Gildas, Colum-

Beda Venerabilis

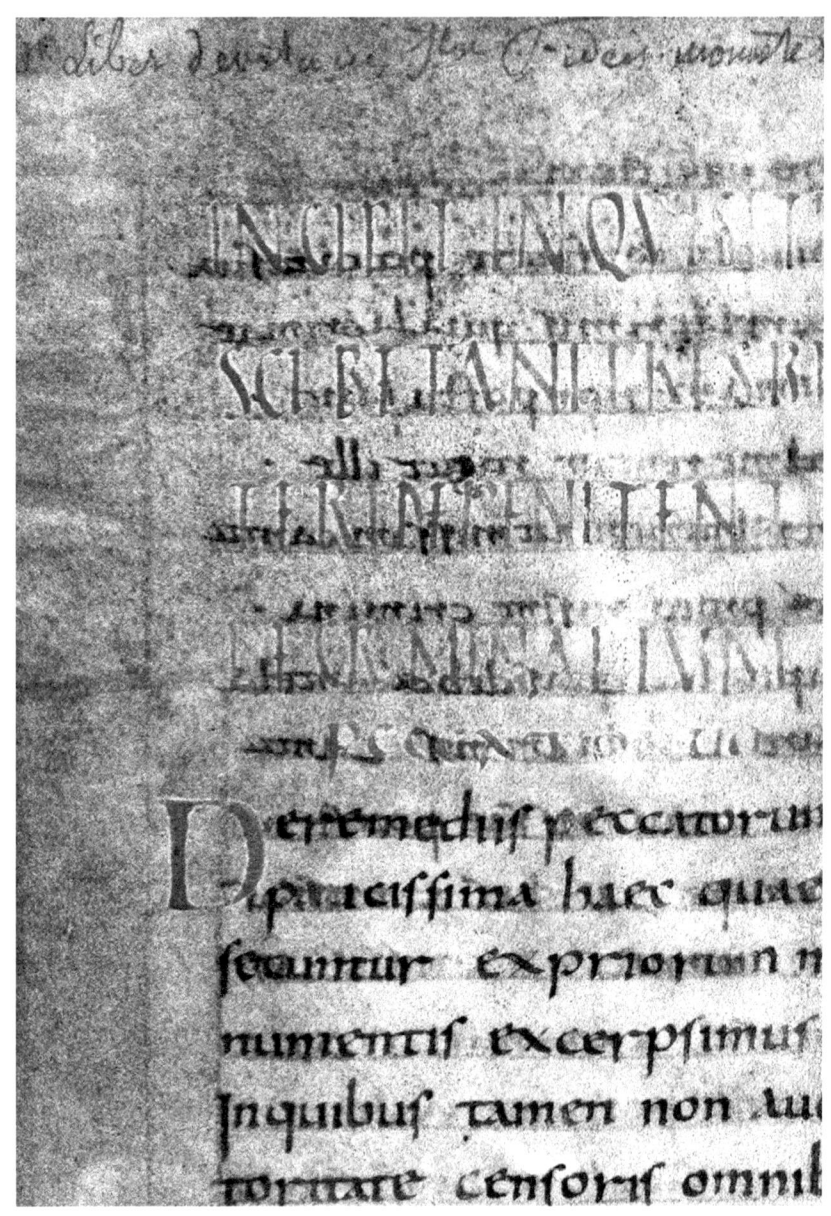

The beginning of Bede's contribution to the
Anglo-Saxon Penitentials.

banus and Bede. All together this compendium is called today "The Anglo-Saxon Penitentials". The following citation originates from Bede's lifetime or even later. Because it deals with heathenism, it is very reasonable, that, although England already was Christianized, heathenism was not completely extinct, as the quote shows:

> **It is indeed not permitted to any Christian man that he practice useless auguries as heathen men do, that is that they believe in the sun and the moon and the stars' course and seek time-auguries to begin their events, nor is gathering herbs permitted with any incantation other than with the Pater Noster and with the Credo or with some prayer that belongs to God. If anyone practice these vain things, he is to cease and confess and fast 40 days, and if he turns again to this idleness then he is to fast 3 Lenten fasts.**
>
> http://anglo-saxon.net/penance/index.php?p=TOEP482_9b

Heathens and heathen practices and also related punishments are repeatedly mentioned in these Penitentials, which apparently means that remnants of Paganism still existed in England between ca. 600 and 1000.

What the Venerable Bede really knew about the Pagan religion of the Anglo-Saxons is a contested issue, and the accuracy of his knowledge of Pagan practices has been questioned occasionally. One of the arguments is that Bede was born after the conversion of England was already officially completed for quite awhile, and Bede was born and raised in a devout Christian family and neighborhood. Hence, apparently, he may have had no first-hand information about the Pagan past. This question also concerns Eostre. However, according to the just mentioned penitentials, it is possible that Bede in his study got detailed knowledge about past heathen times and its remnants in his own time.

Bust of Jacob Grimm, 1881 by Emil Hundrieser

Jacob Grimm and Ostara

Title page of the first edition of Grimm's Teutonic Mythology from 1835

After having brought in Bede as the source for a goddess Eostre in England, the 19th century German scholar Jacob Grimm is mentioned as a second source for the equivalent of Eostre on the European mainland.

The Latin form 'Eostre' which Bede used, is most likely in Old English *Ēostre* and *Ēastre*; while the Old High German form Ostara (**Ôstara*) was proposed by Jacob Grimm in the 19th century, probably derived from

- Germanic *'*austa'*, *'*austra'*: 'eastwards, east of', east',
- Old High German *'ōstar'*: 'in the east', 'to the east';
- Old High German *ōstara*'*, 'Easter, Easter festival'
- Old High German *ōstarmānōd** – name für April (see p. 25).

Grimm concluded a spring and fertility goddess called Eostre or Ostara must have existed.

Here is the English translation of what Grimm actually wrote from Teutonic Mythology, vol. 1. p. 290:

> **The great christian festival, which usually falls in April or the end of March, bears in the oldest of OHG remains the name ôstarâ (gen. -ûn); it is mostly found in the plural, because two days (ôstartagâ, aostortagâ) were kept at Easter. This Ostarâ, like the Anglo Saxon Eástre, must in the heathen religion have denoted a higher being, whose worship was so firmly rooted, that the christian teachers tolerated the name, and applied it to one of their own grandest anniversaries.**
>
> James Stephen Stallybrass translation

Grimm based his "Ostara view" on a linguistic deduction. However, that might be erroneous. In Old High German there is no evidence for such a Pagan goddess among the words he mentioned.

Easter month:
  - Old High German *ōstarmānōd**
  - Old-Saxon **ōstarmānuth?*
Paschal lamb *ōstarfrisking*
Easter day *ōstartag**
Eastern *ōstar*, ōstara*, ōstarūn (pl.)*
  in the east,
    to the east: *ōstar*
  - Germanic **austa, *austra*
Oriental *ōstarling**

The meaning of the name of a goddess for *ōstara was only added in the 19th century to Old High German, after Grimm's publication. It does not exist in OHG from before Grimm. So, Grimm's goddess Ostarâ is most likely his own derivation.

Grimm's second causal argument is, that such a goddess would have existed, because in other languages for the Easter feast, derivations of the old 'pascha' are kept, and only German has the term 'Ostern', like the English Easter.
That argument is mostly rejected now. At first, in the leading Frankish bishopric of Cologne until ca. 750 the name *pāsche* was used for Easter. The bishopric of Mainz on the other hand used a Frankish form of the Old English name Easter: *ôstarun*. That was likely introduced by its famous bishop Boniface who was born, raised and became a priest and a scholar in England, before he moved to the European mainland. It is argued, that Boniface introduced that Frankish form of the Old English name for Easter.
Both names *pāsche* and *ôstarun* for Easter from these bishoprics are recorded repeatedly in Frankish times.
Because Boniface and his people did a lot of missionary work throughout Germany, in which they most likely used their Old English based terms, 'Ostern' became the most widespread, and was taken over eventually in all German-speaking regions.
So, it is really conceivable that the current German name 'Ostern' is directly based on Anglo-Saxon Easter.

Another disputable issue is Grimm's conclusion that Ostara would be a Spring and fertility goddess.

All we know from Bede is that there may have been some celebrations for Eostre in April. Neither a specific date is given for such Pagan feasts nor a specific reason. Placing an Eostre or Ostara festival around the beginning of Spring in March is a modern interpretation that lacks historical or mythological sources. Nonetheless, for a religious Pagan festival that may be irrelevant.

Apparently, Grimm's conclusion for a continental goddess Ostara is in the first place based on Bede's entry about Eostre and his own etymological derivations. In this context, it is quite striking that Grimm did not write a word about older German sources in which the name 'Ostera', in this or another spelling, appeared. There still exist several German sources from the time before Grimm was even born, but unfortunately, no answer can be given anymore as to why Grimm ignored them all.

Saxon transfer

The hypothesis circulates, that the Saxons brought their goddess Eostre? to England as they left their homelands in the north of Germany, starting about halfway through the 5th Century. Based on that view, a similar Saxon goddess (Eostar?, Ostara?) is assumed. Another additional, perhaps less probable, view exists that this goddess was mixed with an indigenous deity from the time before the Saxons came and through insular interactions and intermixing Eostre was accepted as a goddess of Anglo-Saxon and Briton

Pagans. If the Saxons indeed had brought the goddess from the European mainland to England, then a possible connection with the divine Austriahenae mothers (see below), could with some restraint be taken into consideration. It is clear though, that no direct evidence or indications for these suggestions exist. It is only based on the general view, that the Saxons, Angles, and other allied peoples brought their culture, including their deities with them as they migrated to England from the north of Germany and the south of Denmark. Indeed, generally, that is a comprehensible view, the appearance of the god name Woden in Anglo-Saxon literature supports it. However, the lack of further detailed information makes it impossible to substantiate it to other names of deities.

An additional related problem would be to find a satisfying answer to the question of what connection could have existed between the early Saxons in the north of Germany and the region where the Austriahenae votive altar stones from Roman times were found. That region was located at quite a distance more to the south and belonged to Roman territory while the homelands of the Saxons were not.

Reconstruction of an Anglo-Saxon village

"Ostara". By Johannes Gehrt, 1884

Charlemagne and April

In the Frankish Empire since the time of Charlemagne, April was called *ôstarmânôt*, likely related to Old English *eosturmonath*. It is enticing to bring this Frankish month name in connection with a deity Ostara. However, we do not know whether *ôstarmânôt* indeed was based on a heathen past or directly developed from the Christian Easter (German: Ostern).

In fact, it is more likely, that the Christian Easter was the immediate cause. Firstly, this view is based on a section in a biography of Charlemagne. In the VITA KAROLI MAGNI (The Life of Charlemagne), written 817–836 by Einhard (Einhardus ~ 770–840), the translation of Samuel Epes Turner, New York, 1880, in chapter 29 reads:

> **He began a grammar of his native language. He gave the months names in his own tongue, in place of the Latin and barbarous names by which they were formerly known among the Franks. He likewise designated the winds by twelve appropriate names; there were hardly more than four distinctive ones in use before.**
>
> **He called January, Wintarmanoth; February, Hornung; March, Lentzinmanoth; April, Ostarmanoth; May, Winnemanoth; June, Brachmanoth; July, Heuvimanoth; August, Aranmanoth; September, Witumanoth; October, Windumemanoth; Novemher, Herbistmanoth; December, Heilagmanoth.**

He styled the winds as follows; Subsolanus, Ostroniwint; Eurus, Ostsundroni-, Euroauster, Sundostroni; Auster, Sundroni; Austro-Africus, Sundwestroni; Africus, Westsundroni; Zephyrus, Westroni; Caurus, Westnordroni; Circius, Nordwestroni; Septentrio, Nordroni; Aquilo, Nordostroni; Vulturnus, Ostnordroni.

Thus, before Charlemagne introduced *Ostarmanoth* and the other month names, they were in majority called before by their Latin names; *Ostarmanoth* was likely called APRILIS before the name conversion. We do not know whether the name *Ostarmanoth* already was in use at that time, but in Latin documents from that time the month name Aprilis is recorded repeatedly. In addition, in those days the name *Ackermonath* (Field month) was in use; that name did not cover one of the months we know, but partially March and partially April. In a second addition, for the not-Latin names the expression "barbarous names" is used. It does not seem reasonable, that they kept a "barbarous" name.

At any case, it is absolutely not acceptable to think, Charlemagne chose the name of a Pagan deity for April. It also can be rejected that Charlemagne was inspired by the Old English *Eosturmonath*, because Bede, who died about 15 years before Charlemagne was born, wrote, that in England *Eosturmonath* was not used anymore, but rather 'Paschal month' was in use for April.

For verification and eventual one's own translation here is the corresponding original Latin text:

Monument of Emperor Charlemagne at the Old Bridge in Frankfurt, by Jakob Fürchtegott Dielmann, ca. 1845

INCHOAVIT ET GRAMMATICAM PATRII SERMONIS. MENSIBUS ETIAM IUXTA PROPRIAM LINGUAM VOCABULA INPOSUIT, CUM ANTE ID TEMPORIS APUD FRANCOS PARTIM LATINIS, PARTIM BARBARIS NOMINIBUS PRONUNTIARENTUR. ITEM VENTOS DUODECIM PROPRIIS APPELLATIONIBUS INSIGNIVIT, CUM PRIUS NON AMPLIUS QUAM VIX QUATTUOR VENTORUM VOCABULA POSSENT INVENIRI. ET DE MENSIBUS QUIDEM IANUARIUM UUINTARMANOTH, FEBRUARIUM HORNUNG, MARTIUM LENZINMANOTH, APRILEM **OSTARMANOTH**, MAIUM UUINNEMANOTH, IUNIUM BRACHMANOTH, IULIUM HEUUIMANOTH, AUGUSTUM ARANMANOTH, SEPTEMBREM UUITUMANOTH, OCTOBREM UUINDUMEMANOTH, NOVEMBREM HERBISTMANOTH, DECEMBREM HEILAGMANOTH APPELLAVIT. VENTIS VERO HOC MODO NOMINA INPOSUIT, UT SUBSOLANUM VOCARET OSTRONIUUINT, EURUM OSTSUNDRONI, EUROAUSTRUM SUNDOSTRONI, AUSTRUM SUN- DRONI, AUSTROAFRICUM SUNDUUESTRONI, AFRICUM UUESTSUNDRONI, ZEFYRUM UUESTRONI, CHORUM UUESTNORDRONI, CIRCIUM NORD-UUESTRONI, SEPTENTRIONEM NORDRONI, AQUILONEM NORDOSTRONI, VULTURNUM OSTNORDRONI.

The Austriahena goddesses

From the first centuries CE the theonym 'Austriahena' is recorded. Concerning this a citation from Gods of the Germanic Peoples, vol. 1, pp. 86f by the present author reads:

> **Almost 150 votive stones were found, dedicated to the Matronae Austriahenae, called Matronis Austriatium, Matronis Austriahenis and Matronis Austriahenabus. These altars are dated to the end of the 2nd and the beginning of the 3rd century CE. Most of them were found at Morken-Harff; Morken and Harff were places of the Rhine-Erft district in the administrative region of Cologne, which both were given up for the brown coal mining in the Rhenish lignite mining area. The residents of Morken / Harf were resettled in the 1960s in the neighboring town of Kaster.**
>
> **The name of the Matronae is interpreted here as Austriahena, being the divine protectors of the district, or town Austriatium (Austriacum). It is suggested that the people from there were called 'Austriates', but another kind of social group with that name is also a possibility.**
>
> **About the meaning of the name quite a few opinions exist, but the most recent one is also the most convincing:**

Votive altar for the divine Austriahena Mothers

The root word of the name is confirmed Germanic, related to Germanic *austra-*: 'east' or 'eastward'. Perhaps it is also related to Old-Indic *usra-*: 'sparkling', 'vivid', luminous.

According to modern etymological views, these Matronae would be divine protecting mothers for a small district called 'Austriacum', perhaps also a water in that district called 'Austra'... maybe simply a district east of the Roman Capital city of Cologne.

The many archaeological finds there from Roman time make it likely, that at the time a Roman/Germanic settlement was built there and, because of the many dedication stones, there must have lived many people.

The conjectured connection with the goddess Ostara/Eostre does not go beyond speculation, nevertheless, the similarity in the name is striking enough to at least consider an association.

If such an association is accepted, then it could be seen as a piece of circumstantial evidence for an early form of Ostara or respectively Eostre. A next step then could be to speculate about the possible Germanic name of these divine mothers. Many more study is needed though to make such a connection plausible, such as how did this name Austriahena (or its Germanic equivalent) survived at least five centuries and how did it come to England, etc.

The Hindu goddess Usha is assumed in this wooden sculpture from the 18th century

Some possible etymology

The etymology of Eostre isn't conclusively clear but usually three possibilities are proposed:

- it is derived from Indo-European *au̯es-, related to Proto-Germanic *Austrō, and to Germanic *aus-, *ausra-: all meaning 'shine', 'brighten'.
- it is related to Germanic *austa, *austra and Old English éaste: 'east'.
- a relation is suggested with the Greek deity 'Eos', the Roman 'Aurora' and the Indian 'Ushas', all seen as 'dawn goddesses' connected to the red shining morning sky, a deity of the birth of the day.

Perhaps these three alternations are connected to each other as the (red) morning sun appears in the east, but that does not go beyond conjecture.

As a side-note: The Indian deity 'Usha' or 'Ushas' is sometimes brought in relation to Spring and that is used as a 'proof' that Eostre / Ostara would be a Spring goddess. This is most likely wrong; no Hindu source gives clear confirmation for that and it would not fit at all to the climate there. Seasons, as we know them, do not exist on that subcontinent; only higher in the mountains may a similar climate change like in Western Europe be assigned. The only reference to Spring is an etymological theory, a construct that is still in ongoing discussion. (See below).

And another side-note:
Only around the two equinoxes the sunrise is really in the east. During the rest of the year it moves between the northeast and southeast. This is due to the inclination of the Earth's axis and the elliptical orbit around the sun. However, one can only ask whether pre-Christian Pagan cultures were capable of being attentive to that, e.g. through stone settings such as sundials.

Jonathan Slocum in his "Anglo-Saxon Dictionary", University of Texas, Linguistics Research Center in The College of Liberal Arts, Austin, 2009, shows common roots for Easter and Eástre and Ostara:

> **eáster, eástor**; gen. eástres; pl. nom. acc. eástro; gen. eástrena; dat. eástron, eástran [=eástrum]; n: eástre, an; n. I. Easter, the feast of Easter; pascha = GREEK:-- On dæge symbeles eástres (in die solemni paschoe), Lk. Lind. War. 2, 41. Wæs ðære ylcan nihte ðara hálgan Eástrena, ðæt seó cwēn cende dóhtor ðæm cyninge (it was on that same holy night of Easter, that the queen bore to the king a daughter), Bd. 2, 9; S. 511, 28. Æfter twám dagum beóþ eástro (post bĭduum pascha fiet). Mt. Bos. 26, 2. Freóls-dæg, se is gecweden Eástre (a feast day which is called Easter), Lk. Bos. 22, l. II. the passover, paschal lamb; pascha:-- To eástron (for the Easter lamb), Mt. Bos. 26, 17. Đá hí eástron offrodon . . . ðæt ðú eástron ete (quando pascha immŏlābant. . . ut mandŭces

pascha). Mk. Bos. 14, 12. [Ger. M. H. Ger. ostern, f; Ker. óstarun, óstrun: Ottf. óstará, óstoron dea, pascha: A. Sax. Eástre, the goddess of the rising sun, whose festivities were in April. Hence used by Teutonic christians for the rising of the sun of righteousness, the feast of the resurrection, Bd. de Temp. Rat. Works, vol. ii. p. 81: Grimm's Deut. Mythol. 8vo. 1855, pp. 180-183.] eáster, eástor; adj. Easter; paschālis:-- Ðys sceal on eáster-ǽfen (this belongs to easter-even). Rubc. Mt. Bos. 28, I; Notes, p. 577, 28, 1 a. Eáster-tíd (easter-tide or time). Homl. Th. ii. 266, 15, 19, 21. Eáster-mónaþ (easter-month, April), Menol. Fox 142; Men. 72.

A related etymological "Wiki" article is still in discussion and therefore not available in its definite form. A part of it reads:

> One of the most important goddesses of reconstructed Proto-Indo-European religion is the personification of dawn as a beautiful young woman. Her name is reconstructed as Hausōs (PIE *$h_2ewsós$- or *$h_2ausōs$-, an s-stem), besides numerous epithets.
>
> Derivatives of *$h_2ewsós$ in the historical mythologies of Indo-European peoples include Indian Uṣas, Greek Ἠώς (Ēōs), Latin AURŌRA, and Baltic Aušra ("dawn", c.f. Lithuanian Aušrinė). Germanic *Austrōn- is from an extended stem *h_2ews-tro-.

The name *h₂ewsṓs is derived from a root *h₂wes / *a̯ues "to shine", thus translating to "the shining one". Both the English word east and the Latin AUSTER "south" are from a root cognate adjective *aws-t(e)ro-. Also cognate is AURUM "gold", from *awso-. The name for "spring season", *wes-r- is also from the same root. The dawn goddess was also the goddess of spring, involved in the mythology of the Indo-European new year.

http://en.wikipedia.org/wiki/Hausos

Not convincing at all is the hypothesis of the German professor Jürgen Udolphs, who relates the terms 'easter' and German 'Ostern' with North Germanic *ausa, with the meaning 'water fetching' and 'pouring water'. He relates this to the Old West Norwegian term *austra, which has as a minor meaning 'fetching and throwing away the water from the ship's bottom'. He then connects that with baptismal rites.

This is perhaps related to a hand bailer which is still called in Norwegian an *auskjer*, in Swedish *Öskar* and in German *Ösfass*.

Because Eostre and Ostara have a similar common etymological basis, according to Udolphs they also would be related to those rites. However, not only is the 'fetching water' meaning a minor connotation, but also the Norse term *diepan* and the Old High German *toufan* are the common words for "to baptize".

Eos, Greek goddess of Dawn

Votive altar stone of the goddess Hurstrga

Ostara, Ostera, Osta and Eostar on the continent

The Goddess Hurstrga

In 1954 an altar stone from the first Century CE was found in the province Gelderland in the Netherlands in which a goddess Hurstrga is recorded in Latin 'DEAE HURSTRGE'. The meaning of the name of this goddess is not indisputably clear. For the first part of the name a connection with Dutch *horst* (hurst) is proposed, being a parcel of land with shrubs or a grove on it.

In today's Dutch, Hurstrga would be pronounced like 'Oestghra' with a soft hardly audible G still used in the same area of Holland to this day. Phonetically (concerning the sound) this comes very near to 'Ostara', hence, 'Hurstrga' could be seen as an early name for Ostara. However, this suggestion does not go beyond folk or popular etymology, the more so since the Germanic form of the name 'Hurstrjōn' is proposed.

The Dutch researcher Tineke Loojinga interprets Hurstrga as a Batavian goddess who was worshiped as a fertility goddess in a grove or a small hill.

The Osta-Stone

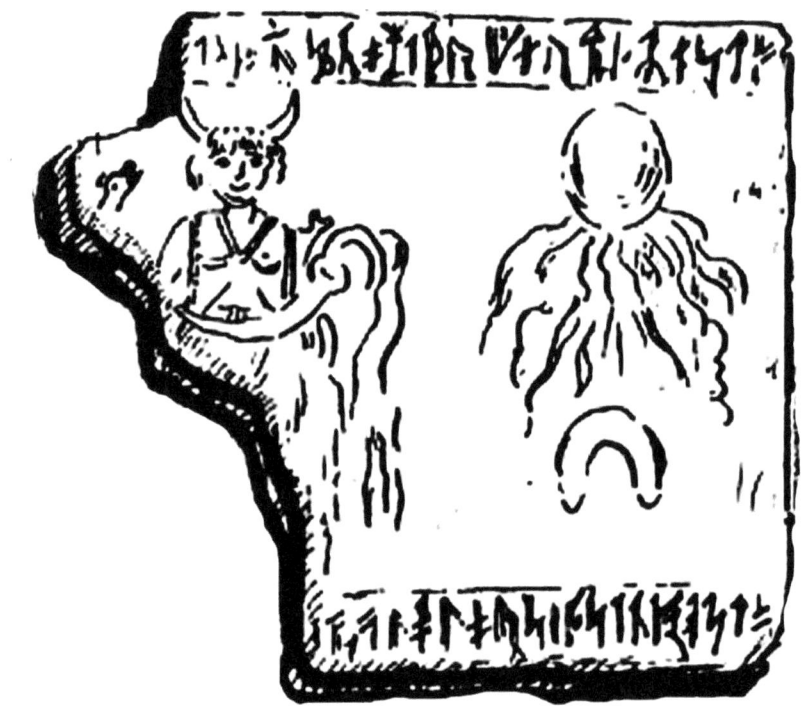

Drawing of the Osta-Stone

In approximately 1590, a votive tablet was found at Hohenstein in the Weser Uplands in Germany. The tablet was made of fired clay and was called "Rune tablet of Hohenstein" and "Osta-Stein" (Osta stone). The depiction is incomplete; it shows a male figure and a female figure who carries a helmet with horns, and a cornucopia. For the runic inscription above and below the depictions three possible translations are offered:

The Runic text transcribed:

dhu gautar osta, ous il sin grosta

Translation 1:   You dear Ostra, from your face it shines ....

Translation 2:   Dedicated to the good Ostra.
(In this second translation the 'dhu' is seen as a dative.)

Translation 3:   The good Osta is coming near.

It is not entirely clear as to whether this sentence is pointing to a goddess or a god. However, because the female figure is presented in more detail and she may have had the central position on the original tablet, a goddess is likely. Accordingly, Osta is interpreted as a shortened form of Ostera or Ostara.

In addition, because the tablet has not survived in its entirety, it is unknown whether the runic text was originally longer; or if indeed at the missing parts on both the top and the bottom runes were also written. It seems likely that if this was the case, then maybe a more intelligible sentence has been lost.

The original has been lost. A replica made of wood, perhaps based on several drawings made from the original, is said to be preserved (still is? where?) in a Marburg Museum. The authenticity of the tablet is disputed, but due to the fact that the original tablet itself cannot be researched anymore, an authenticity debate is pointless. This is all the more so, because it is completely unknown how precise and with what competence or skill the drawings were made.

Although this votive stone is mentioned in several sources, it is striking that none of them writes a word about the possible age of this stone, and hardly anyone points out to which language the transcribed rune sentence can possibly can be attributed. An additional problem is that it is not sure whether the division in the words presented above is correct, because there are no spaces between the runes to divide them into words. Only if these words are accepted, then the language likely points to a regional dialect of Old Saxon. The reply at a request from an expert concerning this confirms this view.

If the tablet is no forgery, then it probably originates from Carolingian times, this perhaps may be restricted to the time the Saxons were still heathen. The conversion of the Saxons to Christianity was completed at least by the early 9th century.

In any case, this tablet is a disputed item. Many do not acknowledge its authenticy; nevertheless, since no unambiguous, decisive arguments for a forgery have been presented yet the objections do not go beyond the level of presumptions or convictions.

Ostara at Osterholz

At the end of the 17th Century, the theologian and historian Ernst Casimir Wasserbach (1664 - 1709), mentions in his "DISSERTATIO DE STATUA ILLUSTRI HARMINII"

nidis affertorum fepulchra. Hic Teutonici montes, Lucos ac nemora confecrata Diis apud *Kolftede* & *fanum Oftera* Deæ prope *Ofterholtz*, *Thietmallum* vetus, & *Schydroburgum* Caroli M. olim hofpitium ad *Ambram*, uti & *Ambronum Cherufcorum* & *Bruēlerorum* pugnaciffimarum *pro libertate*

Fragment from "Dissertatio de statua illustri Harminii"
by Ernst Casimir Wasserbach, 1698

from 1698 a goddess Ostara at the German village Osterholz. The book is a doctoral thesis about a statue of Arminius, also known as Hermann the Cheruscan, the chieftain of the Germanic Cherusci, who revolted against the Romans in 9 CE and defeated a Roman army. Today, Arminius is the commonly used name, but Wasserbach used the Germanized name Hermann. In his introduction, the author also mentions some other antiquities of the extended environment. Among them is a remark about an Ostara sanctuary. The related sentence reads:
LUCOS AC NEMORA CONSECRATA DIIS APUT COLSTEDE ET FANUM OSTERAE DEAE PROPE OSTERHOLZ
This translates as:
Sacred groves and forests dedicated to the gods at Kohlstädt and a sanctuary of the goddess Ostara near Osterholz.

Both the previous villages Kohlstädt and Osterholz are today part of the municipality of Schlangen in the German state of North Rhine-Westphalia, about 17 kilometers

(about 10 miles) south of the statue of Arminius (German: Hermannsdenkmal).
Wasserbach had the reputation of a serious and sincere researcher and author. Fantasy or forgery cannot be attributed to him. Hence, he must have used a source for his Ostera remark which was in his eyes trustworthy enough to use in his thesis. It is possible that he had a source which is no longer available today.

Oostera – Oostera festival

The Dutch work "Schatkamer der Nederlandsse Oudheden" (Vault of Dutch Antiquities) by Ludolph Smids, published in 1711, also contains an entry about the goddess Ostera:

Oostera; weleer een afgodinne der oude Saxen. Ja, deswegen heetmen noch heden, in Westfalen (ik heb het te Munster meer als eens gehoord) de hooge vierdagh van Paschen, het Oosterfeest.

Title page of the "Schatkamer der Nederlandsse Oudheden" by Ludolph Smids, 1711

This translates as:
Oostera, a former Pagan goddess of the old Saxons. Yes, until today because of her in Westphalia (I have heard it more than once when I was in Munster), the high festival of Passover (Easter) is called the 'Osterfest'.

As his source for this the author mentions the German historian Schildius de Chaucis, whose work NOBILISSIMO VETERIS GERMANIÆ POPULO LIBRI DUO (About the Noblemen of the ancient Germanics in two volumes) was first published in 1649 and 1742 the fifth edition had already appeared. Schildius de Chaucis also writes at page 118 of that book:

ITA SAXONES, QUOD BEDAE PRODITUM, OOSTERA QUANDAM IN CLASSEM RETULERANT DEARUM, CUI SACRA QUOTANNIS, APRILI RECURRENTE, ...

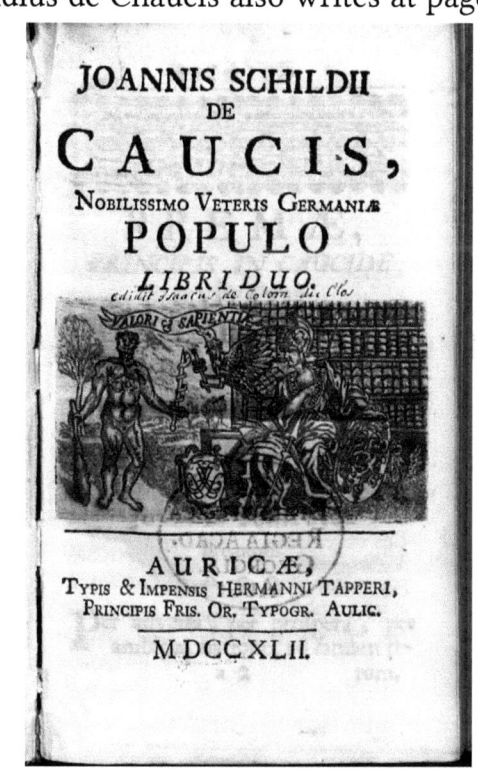

Title page of "Nobilissimo Veteris Germaniæ Populo Libri Duo" by Schildius de Chaucis

Translated rather freely this reads:
> Likewise did the Saxons, as Bede narrated concerning Oostera, which they consider to belong to the group of goddesses, whose annual holy rites recur in April, ...

So, Schildius de Chaucis refers to the related passage by Bede (see above) and he recognizes in a goddess Ostera the continental counterpart of the English Eostre.

De Ostera Saxonum

The historian and author Luneburg Mushard (1672-1708) published in 1700 his book called DE OSTERA SAXONUM (The Saxon Ostera). At page 10 (§ 8) Mushard refers to the already mentioned work by Johann Schildius de Chaucis from 1649, who mentions the goddess Ostera and several of her related place names in Germany.

Mushard himself mentions an older text in which the place Osterholt/Osteralb is called the 'Temple of Ostara'. Citing the related sentence:

> INTER QUAE VEL PRAECIPUUM OSTERAE NENNUS HODIE ETIAM DISTUM OSTER-HOLT/OASTERALB **TEMPLUM OSTERAE**.

This can be freely translated as:
> To this group (of places) which in earlier days were called after Ostera, today also belongs Osterholt / Osteralb with the meaning of "The Temple of Ostera".

alle Mandage de Förste/de Affgaden Priester und dat Volck thosamende/ dar dan Gericht geholden wurd. Ju düssen hilligen Büsche averst mochte nemand gahn / dan alleine de Priester/ und welche de Offerhande dohn wolden. Ock was hier ein Dodschlägerfrig &c. Hæc verba quamvis prolixa potius alleganda videbantur, quam innumera alia aliorum auctorum testimonia, quia in iis tam luculenter lucorum in his regionibus usus depingitur. Sunt enim his terris virgulta adhuc cæsorum lucorum reliquiæ nomen der Hilligen Büsche servantia. Supersunt nomina sacrarum quercuum, juxta quas convenire solebat populus. Uti prope *Bramstedam* erat quercus de Staleke. vid. Schildius de Chaucis l. 1. cap. 12. p. 91. lib. 2. cap. 2. Manent usque in hunc diem nemorum lucorumque sacrorum nomina in his regionibus. Osterwede sylva, quondam spatiosissima, Osterhagen/ Osterndorp &c. Inter quæ vel præcipuum Osteræ nemus hodie etiam dictum Osterholt/Osteralh/Templum Osteræ. ALH enim priscis Germanis templum, inde sine dubio holt/ quia luci & nemora Deorum templa erant; non abludit etiam ab his Græc. ἄλσος, Latinorum *Saltus*. Est eo loco tumulus leniter assurgens in campo olim sine dubio densis arborum umbris cooperto, nunc aperto, nisi quod frutetum restat. In tumulo illo cernuntur ingentium lapidum bini ordines manu ita collocatorum, ut alios majores ordine super impositos sustineant. Tanta magnitudo autem saxorum est, ut vix machinis moveri potuisse videantur. Nihilominus lapis alter superincumbentium extremus, tam affabre quasi à natura factus atque collocatus est, ut altaris satis alti & magni speciem præbeat. Alter autem extremus longe majori mole sepulchralis lapidis præbet imaginem. Hic sacra Osteræ peracta sunt.

§. 9.

Page from Mushards book „DE OSTERA SAXONUM", 1700

Directly before this sentence in the text the place names Osterhagen and Osterdorp and the Osterwede Forest were mentioned.

Beyond this, the book is rather uninteresting. It mainly contains the contemporary views, thoughts and theories about Ostera in which quite a few comparisons are made with Roman, Greek and ancient Oriental deities.

Ostara and Osterode

In DE SAXONUM IDOLO OSTERA (Of the Saxon Pagan Deity Ostera), a chapter of a theological work from 1725, the author Theodorus Hasaeus discusses Ostera. He refers to the Venerable Bede and mentions several places in Germany whose names refer to Ostera, among them again Osterode.

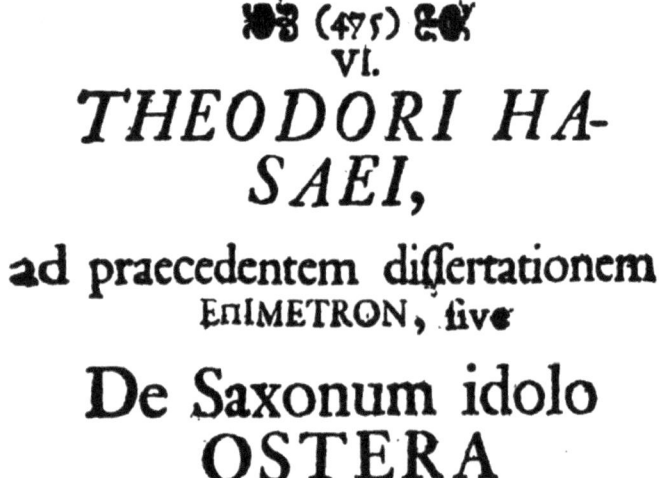

The author, philosopher, historian and teacher Heinrich Pröhle mentions in his book Harzsagen (Myths of the Harz*) from 1859 in his comment about "Zu den Sagen der osteröder Gegend" (concerning the myths of the Osterode region) the goddess Eostar:

> Just for the completeness of all these summaries the short article "The goddess Ostera" is added. It is adapted from the "Osteröder Intelligenzblatt" from 1823, nrs. 29 and 30.
> It preserves the erudite transmission kept in old chronicles which was not included by Honemann and Renner. We are far apart from being able to advocate of what in the text has been said. Casting a glance at the article itself will make that clear.
> "This goddess", as the essay, which is neither signed nor lists any source, reads, "also called Ostra, Ostar and Costar [that has to be Eostar], was especially honored and worshiped by the old Saxons. Even today in Lower Saxony many names of places exist pointing to this goddess, like Osterawald, Osterholz, Osterborn, Osterwiese, Osterbeck, Osterode. At Osterode would have been the main dwelling of the goddess. A grove there was dedicated to her.

---

* The Harz is a low mountain range in Northern Germany and extends across parts of the German states of Lower Saxony, Saxony-Anhalt, and Thuringia. The famous mountain Brocken is with its 3,744 ft the highest peak.

Quite a few other sources from the 18th and 19th centuries exist, all pointing to Osterode as being the main location of the veneration of a goddess Ostara, Ostera, Ostra or Eostar; in addition, concerning this veneration those sources also mention more widely the Harz.

Old picture postcard of Osterode

However, the current view concerning the origin of the name of the town and municipally Osterode does not cohere with the connection described above for the goddess Ostara. As far as it is known, the first written source mentioning that place name dates from 1152: that record reads that the "opulentissima villa Osterroth" was destroyed as the result of a conflict between Henri the Lion and the margrave Albert the Bear of Brandenburg. Yet, it is conclusively known that many centuries before that place was already inhabited.

The name is explained with 'rode' interpreted as 'to clear forest land' and 'Oste' as 'east of'. However, it remains unclear as to what reference in the west this points.

The Sandstone rock formation "Externsteine"

In 1734 the theologian Christoph Friedrich Fein wrote in his treatise on the question put the by the Berlin University as to how far the Romans invaded Germany (Wie weit die Römer in Deutschland eingedrungen), about the veneration of (the goddess) Ostera at the Externsteine. He called that rock formation 'barbaric altars' and also 'EOSTRAE RUPES' (Eostra or Ostara stones). Fein also reports that this German Diana under the name 'Oester' was worshiped in the surrounding forests.

Likewise it was reported in 1762 by the Reverend Pustkuchen from the town Meinberg that the heathen goddess Ostera was worshiped at the Externsteine. About the same time from a nearby Criminal court it was registered, that 'suspicious' rabble was often hanging out at the Externsteine.
This raises the question of whether both things might be related.

Johann Christoph Stübner wrote in his "Merkwürdigkeiten des Harzes überhaupt und des Fürstenthums Blankenburg"

Picture of the Externsteine, ca. 1890–1900

(Curiosities of the Harz generally and of the principality of Blankenburg), volume 1, Halberstadt, 1793, at page 194 (translated):

Horn, an old town in the Lippe region at the Teutoburg Forest, where near the Eoster Stones lie ...

And Johann Heinrich Martin Ernesti reported in his "Miscellaneen zur deutschen Alterthumskunde, Geschichte und Statistik" (Miscellanies to the Germanic Antiquity Studies, History and Statistics), Halle, 1794, at page. 553:

A quarter of an hour before the town [the town Horn is meant, GS] the admirable Externsteine uprise. These are no Magpie stones (PICARUM

RUPES) **but Eoster stones or moon stones** (EOSTRAE RUPES) ...

With that name (EOSTRAE RUPES) the author apparently refers to a further unnamed chronicle from 1750 or to a source from the 16th century.

It is unknown whether that 'Eostra' connection goes back beyond the 16th century. In that and in the subsequent century, several theories about that rock formation saw daylight and it is possible, that this 'Eostra' view was developed at that time too.

Ostera at the Ohlenborg castle

Daniel Eberhard Baring, in his "DESCRIPTIO SALAE" (shortened title) from 1744, also mentions a goddess Ostera. In § LVI, page 59, it reads:

> **Although no remnants of an old castle or other masonry are left here, this is a real possibility, because this vicinity borders the Haynholz [a forest near Hohenstein-Ernstthal, west of the German city of Chemnitz. GS], which borders the Oster forest. The Oster portal of that castle, called Ohlenborg, got its name when in heathen times a sylvan goddess Ostera was venerated and inside that Ohlenborg castle an idolatrous temple would have stood, which was destroyed as**

the Light of the Holy Word arrived there; similarly to the Saxons who had built fortresses and castles to protect their idols.

Title page of the book "Descriptio Salae"

The Zedler Lexicon

The German "Great Complete Encyclopedia of All Sciences and Arts" to which many authors contributed was published by Johann Heinrich Zedler, who had the idea for it and also organized its realization. This multi-volume work was published in the years 1731-1754. Volume 24 contains the following entry:

Ostar, Eostar and Estar were the names of a Pagan deity of the ancient Germanics and particularly of the Saxons. She is the same deity as the one described in the 2nd volume at page 1925f. which is Ostaroth or Astarte. Under the last mentioned name she was actually known among the Germanics.

Title page of the Zedler Lexicon

Title page of volume 3 of the Braga and Hermode" magazine

Braga und Hermode
oder
Neues Magazin
für die
vaterländischen Alterthümer
der Sprache, Kunst und Sitten.

Herausgegeben
von
F. D. Gräter.

Dritter Band.
Erste Abtheilung.

Mit Kupfern und einem Notenblatte.

Leipzig,
bey Heinrich Gräff.
1798.

Starting page of the "Wold and Ostar" article in volume 3 of the Braga and Hermode" magazine

II.

Wold und Ostar,
zwo altteutsche Gottheiten,

von

Karl, Freyherrn v. Münchhausen.
Nebst der Zeichnung eines alten Götzensteines.

a.
Wold.

In Teutschland hat sich, auch selbst in Gebräuchen und Sagen, noch bis jetzt Einiges aus den Tagen der Vorzeit erhalten. Durch Manches blicken sogar noch Ueberreste der alten, fast schier vergessenen Gottheiten hervor und viele Länderstriche Germaniens sind noch voll von Denkmaalen aus dem grauesten Alterthum. Ob ist es das Westphälische, und auch die Grafschaft Schaumburg an der Weser, welche einen Theil von der Heimath der Cherusker und Engern (Angrivari) ausmachte. Man findet da z. B.
V : noch

Münchhausen's "Wold and Ostar"

In his treatise from 1798, Wold und Ostar, zwei altdeutsche Gottheiten (Wold and Ostar, two ancient German deities) by Karl, Freiherr von Münchhausen, this author published his research about 'Ostar' in volume 3 of the German magazine "Brage und Hermode". One of his informants, a minister and "scholar", apparently forgot his scholarly background as he contributed his "knowledge" to the article about the origin of the bonfires at Easter:

> This originates from heathen times. The heathens had an idol called Ostar who in fact was the moon, Luna; the Phoenicians worshiped him under the name Astartes, and the idolatrous Jews as Astaroth. He had the shape of a wench, and wore two horns or a half moon on his head.

This is a quite funny and fanciful view in which even male and female deities are mixed up..

Münchhausen also refers to Johann Weichard von Valvasor (1641–1693), who wrote in his "Die Ehre des Herzogthums Crain" (The Honor of the Dukedom of Crain), Lanbach, 1689, p. 62, about an ancient German idol called 'Easter' and *Æstar* to whom sacrifices were made in April.

Valvasor refers to the Venerable Bede, possibly in combination with an unmentioned German source from which he derived the name *Æstar*.

Page from Valvasor's book

Münchhausen also refers to stories from the 10th and 11th centuries where the moon was worshiped. According to him, that would be Ostar(a), although from those early centuries no specific names of Pagan deities are mentioned. Calling local deities by their indigenous names was not customary at that early time. Münchhausen also mentions possible natural altars for this goddess, among them the Sybillenstein (Sybil Stone) at the place Elstra. He concludes that the older sources he consulted all mention a deity called Ostar and Aster who was venerated in "olden times".

The High-Stone or Sybil Stone at Elstra

Political accommodation

Perhaps an original, but historically most likely wrong view is that of Karl Georg Friedrich Goes, who, in his "The decline of public cult in the Middle Ages", Sulzbach, 1820, mentions

> Following the same maxim, under the Emperor Charlemagne the Spring festival of the goddess Ostera was replaced by the resurrection feast of the Savior of the world, which was called by the name Ostern (Easter), because the Saxons would have been then more disposed towards Christianity.

That means that, according to Goes, the Easter festival (German: Osterfest) got its name to make the Pagan Saxon worshipers of Ostara become more willing to convert to Christianity; hence, the name Ostern (Easter) would have been a political accommodation.

The Blankenburg Oster-Stone

Gustav Klemm in his "Handbuch der Germanischen Alterthümer" (Handbook of German Antiquities) from 1836 reports at p 293, 294:
> A real monument of the ancient veneration of the gods is the Osterstein (Oster Stone) in the Blankenburg region, which is 18 feet high and

40 feet wide and with hewn holes in it. In 1781 there was also found a masonry construction of 30 feet radius whose center is hollow and this was held to be the location of the altar. The Sibill Stone at Elstra has also been related to the worship of Ostar.

East of the castle Regenstein stood the Ostra Stone altar.

Klemm refers to a similar entry in "Merkwürdigkeiten des Harzes überhaupt und des Fürstenthums Blankenburg" (Curiosities of the Harz generally and of the principality of Blankenburg) by Johann Christoph Stübner, volume 1, Halberstadt, 1793, p. 195. This author further explains at page 196 about this Oster Stone:

Osterkirche (Easterchurch) is a place belonging to the sheep farm of the administration of

Stiege, where the oral tradition says that at that place the temple of an idol stood. In 1781 that place was dug off to get debris and stones for roads repair.

So, this altar stone does not exist anymore.

The Corvey 'Eostar' field blessing

Several sources mention a goddess 'Eostar'; the name is widely seen as another name for Ostara. This name is based on a 'medieval' document that once would have been preserved in the monastery of Corvey, located near the city of Höxter in the German state of North Rhine-Westphalia. That document contained a short Old Saxon field blessing poem in which the name of this Goddess is recorded.

Nikolaus Hocker in his "Deutscher Volksglaube in Sang und Sage" from October 1853, is, as far as known, the first one who mentions this field blessing poem. In his comments at the end of the book he writes at p. 224:
In an old song, preserved in the Monastery of Corvey, it reads:
Eostar, Eostar, eordhan modor
(Ostar, Ostar, Erdenmutter) ...

The oldest source which mentions the whole poem is the author Montanus (Vincenz v. Zuccalmaglio). Volume 1 of his "Die deutschen Volksfeste, Volksbräuche und deutscher Volksglaube in Sagen, Märlein und Volksliedern" (The Ger-

Im Kloster Korvei wurde uns noch ein Barden-
chor aus dem altsächsischen erhalten, etwa also lautend:

Eostar Eostar neudeutsch:	Ostar Ostar
eordhan modor	Erdenmutter,
geune these	Lasse diesen
acera vearendra	Acker wachsen,
and virdhendra	Laß ihn grünen,
eacniendra	Laß ihn blühen,
eluiendra	Früchte tragen,
fridha him!	Gieb ihm Frieden!
that his nrdh si gefridhod	Daß die Erde sei gefriedet,
and heo si geborgun	Daß sie sei geborgen,
as his halige	Wie die Heiligen,
the on heof enum sint.	Die im Himmel sind.

Page from the book by Montanus

man Folk Festivals, Folk Customs and Popular Belief in German Myths, Tales and Folk Songs), was published in 1854, apparently only a few months after Hocker's book appeared. In this book Montanus writes at page 28, translated:

> "In the Corvey Monastery a bard choir from Old Saxon was passed down to us, which reads about this:
> Eostar, Eostar,
> eordhan modor,
> geune these
> acera vaxeandra
> and virdhendra,
> eacniendra,
> eluiendra,

fridha him!
That his yrdh si gefridhod,
and heo si geborgun,
as is halige
the on hoef denum sint.

This text reads, corrected according to more current knowledge of Old Saxon near to Anglo Saxon:

Eostar, Eostar,
eordhan modor,
genne these
acera veaxendra
und wirdhendra
eacniendra
einiendra.
fridha him!
that his yrdh si gefridhod
and heo si geborgan
as his halige,
the on heofdenum sind.

Translated:
Eostar, Eostar,
Mother Earth,
let this field
grow and
become green,
let there grow blooms
and fruits.

> Peace to it!
> May its ground be safe,
> And may it be protected,
> like the saints,
> who are in heaven.

Those who accept this text as a valuable old poem assume the age of the original document to be approximately a thousand years old. The Old Saxon language is documented from the 9th until the end of the 11th century. Based on the words used in the poem it may originate from the 10th century. Perhaps it existed earlier orally.

Reading more carefully the exact words of Montanus, it seems reasonable to accept that he did not have the original document at his disposal, but possibly a transcript which he considered to be not completely correct.

As a side note: the same poem can be found at page 30 in "Deutsche Pflanzensagen" (German Plant Myths) from 1865 by Anton Ritter von Perger, a professor and librarian at the Royal Library (Hofbibliothek) at Vienna.

The original document of the Corvey monastery apparently does not exist anymore. That loss perhaps happened during the Thirty Years' War in Central Europe, because at that time the Benedictine monastery founded in 822 was heavily damaged at the big 'Monastery-fire', also called the 'slaughter of Höxter' in 1635. For the most part the monastic library also was destroyed. The just mentioned transcript might have been written down from memory by a monk who may have had good knowledge of the document. However, such a copy is not available. Yet, the view sometimes expressed that the medieval document never existed is a less probable conjecture. The disappearance of documents from the Middle Ages is unfortunately no rarity

Westwork Corvey Abbey; the only part of the Abbey left after the fire in 1635.

- from quite a few of them we only know of their previous existence because other remaining works refer to or contain citations of them.

From the late 10th or early 11th century, at about the same time the Corvey document is dated, a ritual is preserved in Anglo Saxon England which can make a field fruitful again prior to sowing. This Æcerbot Ritual is longer than the Eostar poem, but it shows a remarkable similarity. In fact, so many identical words are used that a connection between the two poems is very likely. But what that connection could be does not go beyond guessing. Some suggestions are:

- The Old English Æcerbot Ritual was the 'template' for the Corvey poem.
- The Corvey poem was the 'template' for the Æcerbot Ritual which then was expanded with the other parts.
- Both were written by the same person. (Monks indeed traveled frequently enough between England and the Continent to make such a possibility reasonable).
- A rather devious view sees the Corvey document as 18th century forgery for which the Æcerbot Ritual was used as a template.

The Æcerbot Ritual and the Corvey poem side by side:

Part of the Æcerbot-Ritual	The Corvey poem
Erce, Erce, Erce, eorþan modor.	Eostar, Eostar, eordhan modor,

Part of the Æcerbot-Ritual	The Corvey poem
Geunne þe se alwalda,	genne these
ece drihten	
æcera wexendra	acera veaxendra
and wridendra,	und wirdhendra
eacniendra	eacniendra
and elniendra, sceafta hehra,	einiendra.
scirra wæstma,	
and þæra bradan	
berewæstma,and þæra hwitan	
hwætewæstma, and ealra	fridha him!
eorþan wæstma.	that his yrdh si gefridhod
Geunne him, ece drihten,	and heo si geborgan
(and his halige	as his halige,
þe on heofonum synt),	the on heofdenum sind.
þæt hys yrþ si gefriþod	
wið ealra feonda gehwæne,	
and heo si geborgen	
wið ealra bealwa gehwylc,	
þara lyblaca	
geond land sawen.	
Nu ic bidde ðone waldend	
se ðe ðas woruld gesceop,	
þæt ne sy nan to þæs cwidol	
wif, ne to þæs cræftig man	
þæt awendan ne mæge	
word þus gecwedene.	
Hal wes þu, folde,fira modor!	
Beo þu growende on godes	
fæþme, fodre gefylled,	
firum to nytte.	

To complete this section here is the translation of the related part of the Æcerbot field blessing, taken from "The Nerthus claim" by the present author, Norderstedt 2012, p. 124f:

> Erce, Erce, Erce,
> earth's mother,
> May the all-ruler grant you,
> the eternal lord,
> fields growing and flourishing,
> propagating and strengthening,
> tall shafts, bright crops,
> and broad barley crops,
> and white wheat crops,
> and all earth's crops.
> May the eternal lord grant him,
> and his holy ones,
> who are in heaven,
> that his produce be guarded
> against any enemies
> whatsoever,
> and that it be safe
> against any harm at all,
> from poisons [lyblaca]
> sown around the land.
> Now I bid the Master,
> who shaped this world,
> that there be
> no speaking-woman [cwidol wif]
> nor artful man
> [craeftig man] that can overturn

these words
thus spoken.
Whole may you be
[Be well] earth,
mother of men!
May you be growing
in God's embrace,
with food filled
for the needs of men.

The Gambach 'Oistirsteynen'

At Gambach, formerly a place in its own right, today the largest district of the town of Münzenberg in the German state of Hesse, in 1351 a field name was recorded as *Osterveld*, in 1363 as *Ostirveld* and in 1403 as *uff dem Ostirfelde* (at the Oster-field). The rock formation at that field was documented in 1403 as *an den Oistirsteynen* (at the Oster-stones). In 1845 most of the rock formation at that field was blown up to use the stones as building material.

In 1853 the German scholar of Germanic studies and author Johann Wilhelm Wolf gives some details in his work "Beiträge zur deutschen Mythologie 1: Götter und Göttinnen" (A Contribution to German Mythology 1: Gods and Goddesses). He refers to a work of 1847 in which that rock formation is described quite detailed. That description narrates that:

... the top of it is not naturally formed; it looks flattened by humans and contains small ditches;

it all looked as if the place in earlier times was used as a sacrificial altar. After the rocks were blown up, a mixture of soil and ashes was found, which obviously points to fires in the past. One of the cracks in the rocks was called "der Backofen" (the oven) by the local people.

The author also mentions a piece of lore around that stone. At Easter, boys from two neighboring villages ran to the rocks with the aim of getting on the top first. During the footrace they tried to slow down the boys from the other village by throwing stones at them. This competition is interpreted by Wolf as symbolizing the eternal annual battle between winter and summer.

Current remnants of the Gambach Easter Stones

Because of the name of the field and of the rock formation and the artificial processing of the top, a cult place for the heathen Goddess Ostera/ Ostara is interpreted by several authors; a former Pagan cult place would indeed be possible here.

Forms of Easter in names of places and people

Very old names of places, waters and of peoples who lived long ago, were and are often seen as indications for the worship of some deity. It should be kept in mind that this is often a delicate and concerning many names also a contested form of evidence.

Concerning Eostre, linguists reconstructed the word **auster* and that is often considered as a potential early form of the deity name Ēostre.

In the year 702 or 703, King Aldfrith of Northumbria called a court, known as "The council of Austerfield". The Latin sentence reads:
IN CAMPO QUI EOSTREFELD DICITUR" AND "IN CAMPO QUI DICITUR OUSTRAEFELDA
(at a field that is called Austerfield).

This place is identified as Austerfield near Yorkshire. This place name is brought in connection with 'ēoster' and accordingly also with the goddess Ēostre.

Other place names in Britain which are also brought in connection with this theonym are Eastry in Kent, Estrey

King Aldfrith of Northumbria

in Cambridgeshire and Eastrington near Yorkshire. However, these assumptions do not have a solid base. Also it is unknown whether those place names originate from Pagan times. Of the ones mentioned here, the oldest one is Eastry which was recorded in 788 as Eastrgena.

In Germany place names like Osterholz, Osterode and Austerthal are sometimes indirectly brought in connection with Ostara, or Ostera.

It has to be stated though that there are many names of places with the term 'east' or the German term 'Ost' in some form as part of it, and in any case those which are recorded for the first time from after ca. 900 CE do not point to a Pagan deity but are connected with direction, e.g. situated east of some other place or of a river, etc.

In several human names the word *ēoster* is also identified. The name *Easterwine* is recorded as the name of a 7th century abbot. It is also recorded several times for other people. *Easterwulf* is another example for a male name. And the female name *Aestorhild* might be an early form of the later Estrild. For names from the European mainland, such as *Austrechild, Austrighysel, Austrovald* and *Ostrulf* a similar religious connection is assumed.

Several scholars think they recognize in the names of the different kinds of places which carry or point to the name of a deity, an ancient (Germanic) habit, that had already been described in the year 98 CE by the Roman historian

Tacitus. Chapter 9 of his ethnographic essay "Germania" ends with the words:
LUCOS AC NEMORA CONSECRANT DEORUMQUE NOMINIBUS APPELLANT SECRETUM ILLUD, QUOD SOLA REVERENTIA VIDENT.
This is translated as:
They consecrate woods and groves, and give the names of the deities to that mysterious something which only the eye of reverence can see.

This is interpreted to mean, that those sacred places carried the name of the deity, who also was worshiped there. Especially the Saxons would have kept that tradition until their conversion to Christianity.

Perhaps it is superfluous, but nonetheless it has to be pointed out that such name connections with the goddess Eostre or Ostara perhaps point solely to a common linguistic root. In almost all cases it is not verifiable that those names came directly or indirectly from these deities.

Nevertheless, it is important to realize that the terms 'Easter', and German 'Oster', 'Ostre', 'Ostra' do appear in names at all. Place names can be named after a deity, personal names can point to a deity; but people do not worship a wind direction or the name of the direction of a specific quarter. Hence, the conclusion seems to be allowed and credible that, when feasts are celebrated in honor of Eastre, Eostre, Ostre, Ostera or Ostara (in this or in another notation), the name refers to a person or a deity

den. Oftera komme aber her von Oft und Ar, welches auf Gothisch das Jahr bedeutet, und erkläret es durch unser Frühjahr oder Vorjahr. Der daselbst angeführte Herr von Leibniß, hält nichts wahrscheinlicher, als, daß durch Eoftra die Morgenröthe verstanden werde, indem Oft bey den Deutschen der Aufgang heisse, bey den Engelländern: East, bey den Italiänern Oftro; in dem Märzmonat aber, (da gedachte Göttin verehret seyn soll) und um die Zeit, da Tag und Nacht im Frühling gleich, die Sonne recht im Aufgange sey. In der neuen Vorrede zur dritten Auflage von 1737. wird auf der neunten

Explanation about the origin of Ostera from "Historically-dogmatic treatise of the fixed public holidays and Sundays", page 35, by Dietrich A. von Stade 1795

Easter Day itself has gathered fewer folk traditions. Many people followed, and still follow, the rule of wearing at least one new article of clothing (frequently a pretty hat) when going to church that morning. The customary food was roast lamb and mint sauce, in allusion to the Passover Lamb with its garnishing of bitter herbs. As for the charming belief that the sun, at its first rising on Easter Day, dances in the sky in honour of the resurrection, Sussex people in the nineteenth century had a variant of their own – they did indeed hold that the sun danced, but they added that nobody would ever see it, 'because the Devil is so cunning that he always puts a hill in the way to hide it'.

A piece of Easter lore from "The Folklore of Sussex" by Jacqueline Simpson, London, 1973.

Tradition and folklore

To state it straight directly at the beginning of this chapter ...
except for Bede's general remark, that in April feasts were held in honor of Eostre, there are no customs, traditions or lore that can be positively attributed to the goddess Eostre or Ostara. For many of them only the general remark can be made, that they perhaps could have been part of a Pagan culture on the European mainland or in England, because
- they generally would fit to natural religions;
- they are recorded in other ancient Pagan cultures;
- they fit with annual seasonal characteristics.

All of the following examples were (some still are) practiced inside Christianity and they were part of Christian lore and customs. It can only be a matter of a personal view to also presume an earlier Pagan connection in them. But then, most of the Easter lore may deal with Spring, with the awakening of nature, with the newly cultivated fields and with the fertility of flora and fauna. Those things are not specific for one religious culture, they almost certainly will have existed in Europe in pre-Christian times. In addition, many customs do not show any apparent connection with the Christian Easter or with Christianity generally. For the effectiveness of Christianity, it was a matter of course to assimilate parts of the local or regional lore and traditions and if appropriate to reinterpret them.

Having made this clear, although there is hardly evidence, not even clear indicators, it is well accepted, that much related lore and customs we know from the Christian Medieval times had their counterparts in heathen times. Hence, it is not far-fetched to assume that quite a few of the lore and customs described here and elsewhere were in some form taken over during the Christian conversion, most likely reinterpreted, and perhaps also somewhat altered, according to the religious acceptance and the cultural and social changes of times. Other customs again may have been developed during the last few centuries and originate from inside Christianity. In some cases these are adopted into current Paganism.

The following short list of lore, traditions and customs is restricted to the British Isles, Germany, the Netherlands and Belgium. Of course many other countries have similar or different practices, but including them would go far beyond the scope of this publication. Additionally, this list is far from complete, it is just an exemplar for much other more or less Easter-related lore, as a look in some of the sources below may show.

Easter Bunny, Easter eggs

Although the Easter Bunny and Easter eggs often are brought in relation to a Pagan Eostre or Ostara festival, it is likely that they probably are not of ancient western European Pagan origin as far as it concerns Germanics and probably also Celts.
 The Easter Bunny was mentioned for the first time in

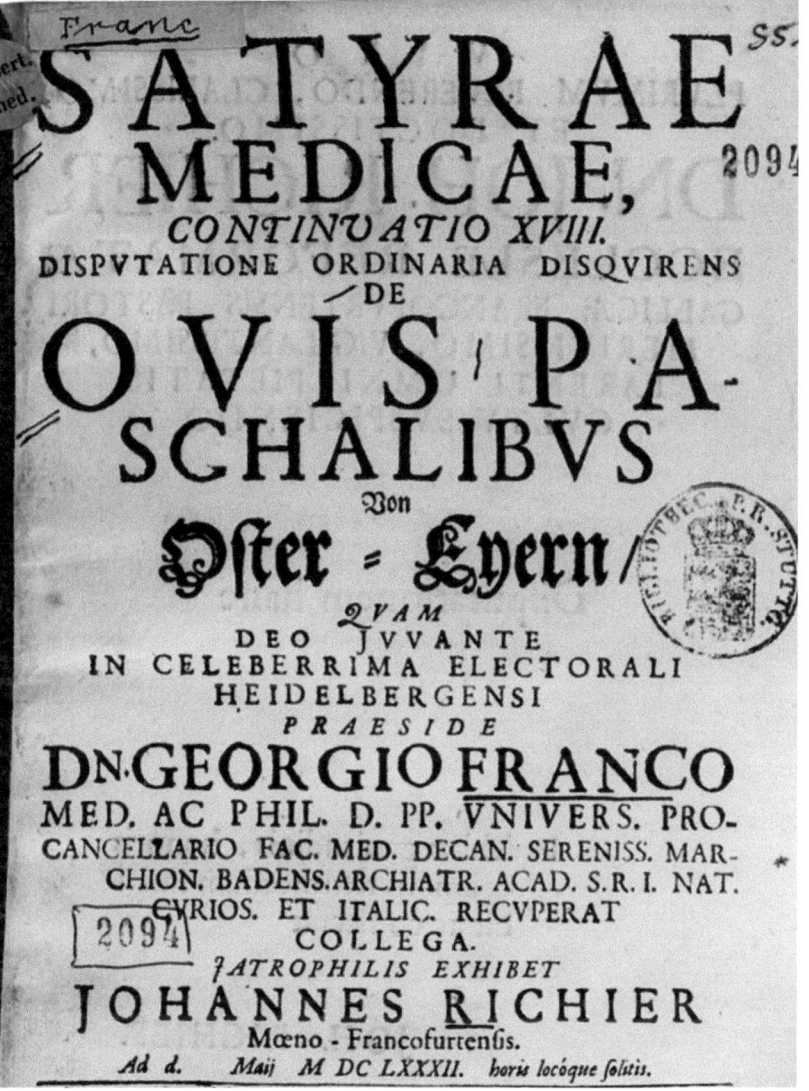

Title page of "De Ovis paschalibus" (Of Easter Eggs)

1682 by Professor of Medicine Georg Franck of Franckenau in his treatise "DE OVIS PASCHALIBUS - (Of Easter Eggs)" He described for regions in the southwest of Germany and bordering French regions the custom of hiding Easter eggs in gardens where they are found by the children, watched by delighted and amused adults. That those eggs would be hidden by an Easter Bunny the author calls a fable, meant for simple men and the children. In the 19th Century German immigrants brought that egg-hiding tradition to the United States, including the "Bunny-fable".

It is even quite possible, that the Easter Bunny in the western cultures is of Christian origin. From the Middle Ages, a multifarious Christian hare symbolism is known, e.g. shown in many paintings while already in the 4th Century CE, in Italy, Saint Ambrose pointed to the hare as a resurrection symbol.

The egg itself appears in many ancient religions and old myths around the world, for example, in Egypt, China, India and Greece. The breaking of the eggshell and the appearance of a new life from inside it are often seen as a symbol and allegory for coming-into-being. Already quite early, this was associated with the incarnation myth of Jesus Christ.

In many traditions around the world the egg is connected to initiation rites, fertility feasts and agricultural rituals. Christianity also knows older and more recent egg-related lore and customs. From Celtic and Germanic Pagan times no old records exist which could indicate that the Celts and

Germanics knew a similar egg symbolism, especially, since poultry keeping only was spread after it was introduced by the Romans in their occupied territories.

That does not mean that eggs did not have a place in their religious life, it does just means we have no reliable information about it.

Easter bonfires

Easter bonfire in Weende, a district of the German town Göttingen.

During the Middle Ages church leaders in many districts interdicted the bonfires at Easter because it was considered a heathen remnant. Despite their attempts, a complete extinction failed. From 1342 a record has been passed down about a Count at Hörde (previously a town, today a district of the city Dortmund in Germany), that admitted the people to a hill at his estate to burn Easter bonfires.

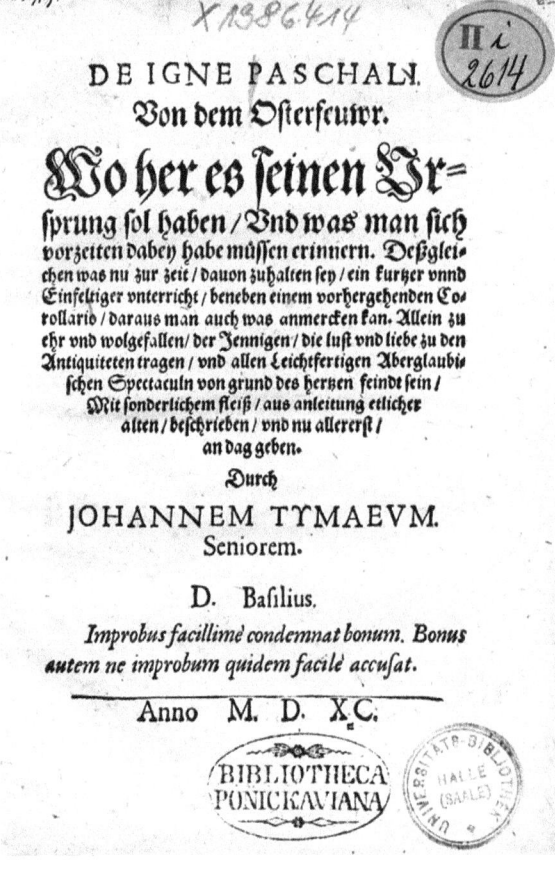

Title page from the book book "Vom Osterfeuer" (About the Easter Bonfire) by Johannes Timaeus from 1590.

Johann Timaeus in his book Vom Osterfeuer (About the Easter Bonfire), Hamburg, 1590, described how people in the region of the German towns Brunswick, Lünel and Hildesheim had Easter bonfires on hills, and around the fires the people amused themselves with music, dancing and games. After the feast people jumped over the fire and also cattle were driven through the ashes.

These pieces of lore may be reasonably well accepted as left remnants of Pagan times, pointing perhaps indeed to a goddess Ostera, Ostra, etc.

At least until the 17th century many leading people of the clergy repeatedly complained about the 'disturbances of the shameful and scandalous Easter bonfires'.

The online "Catholic Encyclopedia" gives the following entry about Easter bonfires. As a main source, the German researcher of lore and customs Reinsberg-Düringsfeld (1822 - 1876), is used:

The Easter Fire is lit on the top of mountains (Easter mountain, Osterberg) and must be kindled from new fire, drawn from wood by friction (nodfyr); this is a custom of Pagan origin in vogue all over Europe, signifying the victory of spring over winter. The bishops issued severe edicts against the sacrilegious Easter fires (Conc. Germanicum, a. 742, c.v.; Council of Lestines, a. 743, n. 15), but did not succeed in abolishing them everywhere. The Church adopted the observance into the Easter ceremonies, referring it to the fiery column in the desert and to the Resurrection of Christ; the new fire on Holy Saturday is drawn from flint, symbolizing the Resurrection of the Light of the World from the tomb closed by a stone (Missale Rom.). In some places a figure was thrown into the Easter fire, symbolizing winter, but to the Christians on the Rhine, in Tyrol and Bohemia, Judas the traitor.

Johannes Letzner reports in his "Historia S. Bonifacij, Der Teutschen Apostel genandt" (The history of St. Boniface, Called the German Apostle) from 1602:

After the conversion as these people became Christian, at that same hill on Easter Day at sundawn a bonfire was held which was called in earlier times Bocksthorn.

For his remark, Letzner gives as his authority the Benedictine monk and historian Conradus Fontanus of Huxar who lived in the 13th century.

The name 'Bocksthorn' is discussed quite a few times. It could mean the pile of brushwood for the bonfire, or in another view it is assumed that it points to the old habit of driving the cattle through the ashes of the bonfire.

About this 'thorn' or 'horn', the German historian and author Christian August Vulpius has a different perspective. In his "Curiositäten der physisch literarisch artistisch historischen Vor- und Mitwelt" (Curiosities of the Physical, Literary, Artistic, Historical Primeval and Medieval World), Volume 2, page 458f., from 1812, he writes, thereby referring to the dissertation "De antiq. Goslar. tutelaribus Mar., Simone et Judah Thadd. ac Matt." from 1706 by Johann Michael Heineccius:

It was indeed a big and holy horn which was especially used in the veneration ceremonies of the goddess Ostera. It was kept at certain safe places in the Harz mountain range (where this

goddess was worshiped primarily), and many places carry that 'Horn' in their names, as in the Bremen region Heilshorn, Bogshorn i.e. God's Horn, in the Lüneburg region, Mahnhorn i.e. Horn of Mahns which is the moon. That curved horn form of the moon also represents the Holy Horn, because the goddess Ostera was venerated as the moon.

Anyway, Letzner tells that Easter bonfires already were held in the time of Boniface (673-755) and apparently such bonfires also took place before the conversion of those people. However, Letzner does not relate this to a goddess Ostar or Ostara, but to a Saxon deity called 'Reto', whose altar would have been destroyed by Boniface. The conjecture exists that this deity Reto could be associated in some way to the goddess Hretha, whom Bede mentions.

Although it may be accepted as correct that bonfires generally were part of many Pagan customs in various regions of the world, no clear evidence exists about heathen bonfires at the Spring Equinox from pre-Christian times in western Europe. The first Easter-related bonfire is reported to come from France around 750 CE - however, if Letzner's entry is correct, then Easter bonfires were held earlier in Germany, at least as early as the time of Boniface.

Easter bonfires are known in several countries. In some places throughout the year, people gather and bring branches, twigs and other natural combustible things to their place of fire. Both specific Christian and Pagan interpretations for these bonfires are circulating: the huge bonfires symbolize the essence of life, and they would ensure fertility, growth and a bountiful harvest. Or they are also seen as a symbol of Christ's resurrection.

The day the Easter bonfire is held varies from place to place; some are lit at the Saturday before Easter, others in the evening of Easter Sunday.

In many places, people not only stand in a circle around the fire, they also sing and dance and have fun. That should express the delight of welcoming the summer, or, from a Christian point of view, the delight of the forthcoming return of Christ.

More Lore, Customs and Traditions

At least on the day before Easter, potatoes and parsley should be sown or planted.

Playful activities are organized on the day before Easter both for adults and for children. These are presumed to be remnants of old fertility rituals for the cultivated fields and kitchen gardens.

In earlier times new soldiers were initiated at Easter. This is supposed to continue the ancient custom of not fighting battles in winter, and in early Spring setting the troops on stand-by again.

Hot cross buns were (and still are) especially eaten in the time before Easter, at some places during Lent before Eas-

Hot cross buns

ter. At other places they aren't eaten but hanged near the hearth or at some other central place, which would bring luck for a whole year. Some people bake them at Good Friday, because only then would the buns have protective power and could cure many illnesses.

Because of the cross on the buns, at first sight, it looks like purely Christian lore. However, similar cakes with a cross on them were already known in ancient Pagan Greece. Sun-crosses are documented from many ancient cultures around the world, going back to the Stone Age. The conjecture, that sun-crosses were part of pre-Christian Germanic or Celtic cultures, perhaps also symbolizing the returning power of the sun in Spring is not far-fetched.

Processions are held. Some are only for boys, others for children or for adults. Some make loud noise to drive out winter, others carry torches symbolizing the increasing strength of the sun, the increasing daylight towards summer and, of course, symbolizing the resurrection of Christ.

Coloring eggs at or shortly before Easter is an ancient tradition. While the egg itself symbolizes life, the different colors have meanings too: gold-colored ones stand for preciousness, green for the herbal nature, etc.

Many kinds of games with eggs exist, like
- rolling them down the slope of a hill (the egg that rolls the longest distance wins).
- throwing eggs over the roof of a house (their shells should not break).
- throwing eggs at the egg of someone else who is holding it in the hand (with the aim of breaking the other's while keeping one's own unbroken).
- In a variation, the eggs are kept in the hand and two people push their eggs together; the winner is he whose egg does not break at hitting.

Of course, these eggs are all hard-boiled before.
In another egg-game someone holds a hard-boiled egg between their forefinger and thumb. An opponent tries to toss a coin into the egg. If the coin gets stuck, he wins the

egg. If the coin falls down, the egg-holder wins the coin. The game is rather painful for the egg-holder, because the thrown coin can quite hurt the bones of the fingers.

Another custom is to blow out raw eggs and then paint them with miniature graphics. That has become a tradition in many countries. As motives miniature depictions or ornamental adornments are customary. This has grown to a real art and those jewelry eggs are then often exhibited.

Decorated Easter eggs

If a debtor pays his debt before or at Easter, he is a free man again; this is compared to the hare who is not rushed by the dog. At some places the payment should also contain some (colored) eggs.

Ground altar for a Pagan Ostara ritual a few years ago.

The custom of 'Easter-laughing' is still an active piece of lore. It is symbolic for freeing the mind after hearing a sermon about the suffering of Christ. It is assumed this represents an older tradition of eliminating the overwhelming difficulties of winter and welcoming Spring. At Easter people come together in groups where funny stories or jokes are told, a traditional way to activate this laughter.

When two people jump over a (small) bonfire together, they either will get married within a year, or, if they are already a couple, she will become pregnant within a year.

Glowing charcoal from the bonfire is brought into the houses of the villagers; that will give protection against hail, lightning or livestock diseases.

Men with torches walk through the streets, play instruments (shawns, zithers, etc.) while singing. They are followed by children who carry baskets in which they collect eggs, or bread and wine, or firewood for the bonfire.

At Easter Sunday at some places the boys take buckles off from the girls. And at Easter Monday the young women take off the boys' shoes and buckles. At the Wednesday after Easter these things were given back against a small forfeit; this was then used to have a 'tansy-cake' party together with dancing.

Groups of young males performed a play of a formalized battle, in which death and its revival are highlighted. This is presumed to symbolize the return of life in nature after triumphing over winter.

Around Easter, running contests for the young people were held in the fields, sometimes bare-foot and over wet grass. The prize for the winner is a cake.

A shoe donation, please, for the Easter Festival.

At Easter Monday, neighboring villages organize bottle-kicking contests, which possibly may have had a heathen equivalent.

Another custom is described as follows:

> It follows a hare-pie scramble that may go back to the Saxon Easter-hare rites, but it is said to date from a bequest made centuries ago of a piece of land to the rector on condition that he and his successors provides annually two hare-pies, 'a sufficiency of ale' and two dozen penny loaves to be scrambled for on Easter Monday ...
>
> Roy Christian

Hare pie

Windows were decorated with Easter eggs that were strung on threads. The people with the window that showed the most eggs became Easter King or Queen.

Because in many cultures water is seen as a life-giving element, at Easter also customs are practiced that deal with water.

- Between midnight and daybreak of Easter Sunday morning, fresh water is scooped from a stream or a creek and carried home in silence. For the whole year it should cure eye diseases, rash and other smaller diseases, and it also ensures youth and beauty until the next Easter.
- To ensure their fertility, young women silently scoop water against the flow of the stream and drink it in the next days. During that scooping and until the water is brought and stored inside the house, the silence must not be broken. Only then the water keeps its blessing and healing powers. And no drop of water should be lost or drip, both on the way and at the home of the girl.
- To show the thankfulness for the life-bringing water, at Easter fountains are beautifully decorated with gar-

At Easter Monday in Tenby (Wales) at sunrise the inhabitants cast three somersaults, celebrating the resurrection of Christ or the return of life in nature.

Afterword – Some Final Remarks

In a first concluding remark it should be pointed out, that today with our central heating systems, with enough food and fresh fruit throughout the year and similar luxuries, we can hardly imagine anymore what a relief and joy it was in earlier days when Spring came back. In the houses, where in winter the glassless windows at best could be closed with pigs' bladders and in times of frost were stuffed with straw, fresh air and light could return inside in Spring, and pinewood chips, oil lamps and torches could be doused. Coldness, darkness and hunger came to an end. Fresh herbs could be cut in the fields, chickens started laying eggs again and newborn male goats could be slaughtered to get fresh meat. (Originally, the Passover roast was a goat lamb).

Based on such life conditions, many customs have their explanations, regardless of the additional religious contents, be they Christian or Pagan. Easter (Ostern) is a festival of joy! It is a matter of a personal Pagan religious view whether that festival in Spring had a goddess Eostre or Ostara as its patroness.

Related to this last sentence, an explanation might be appropriate concerning the remark from the foreword:
"A religious view concerning such a goddess does not necessarily need the information provided here."
It may have been noticed, that the author has avoided drawing a conclusion as to whether there was a goddess Eostre or Ostara in Pagan times. The most important reason for this is that there is no reliable detailed historical

information about the actual religious practice of the Pagan Germanic peoples. Sure, we have myths, folk tales, customs and extremely sparse historical comments; but that is not enough to determine with fair certainty that any Germanics at whatever early era worshiped this goddess and sacrificed to her. For a heathen religious acceptance of Ostara or Eostre historical, mythological or other scientific results of research are unnecessary. Generally, no god and no goddess is provable in these ways, with scientific methods, regardless the concerned religion. For that no science is needed, it takes faith.

Finally there is another thing to consider, perhaps after this book is finished. During the reign of Charlemagne, many Pagan artifacts and cult places were destroyed or incorporated in some way in the course of Christianization. These were in particular those which were known regionally, or were clearly discernible. However, local places of worship which mainly had been chosen because of their natural conditions, apparently were not targeted by the early church leaders, perhaps, because it was easier to keep them secret.

But after the descriptions of such places appeared in the literature of the Renaissance and were even amplified in the Romantic Age, these places came to the attention of a wider community. The question can be put seriously, whether the destruction of such places since the 18th century, was indeed only justified by a need of building materials, or if it had a similar (hidden) religious motive. A similar question of an exertion of influence from the church can be posed concerning the reports and notes of the disappearance in whatever way of heathen artifacts and documents from the Middle Ages.

It has to be stated, that not all old sources in which is written about 'Ostera' were cited. Between 1500 and 1900 many shorter and longer contributions about this goddess name and generally about Pagan deities in Germany were published. Quite a few of them were reactions or reviews concerning publications of others. To give an example:
The teacher, theologist and university preacher Christian Wilhelm Flügge (1772 - 1828) at Göttingen (Germany), wrote a longer article "Über die Ostera der alten Sachsen" (About the Ostera of the old Saxons), published 1796. He presents nothing that could add something new or interesting to this book. He refers to Bede, sees connections with related place names, draws links to Greek deities, etc. In another article he wrote a critical review about the here earlier presented "Wold and Ostar" article by Münchhausen.

And in 1805 Friedrich Rühs published his scorching review about Flügge's article in which all what Flügge wrote about Ostera is disbelieved.

Adding these and many more similar sources would at least have doubled the size of this book and would make it also deadly boring.

Easter fountain in the German municipality of Mudau

Gratitude is expressed to ...

Researching and writing 'something' about Ostara was since 2007 at my TODO list and since that time the process of gathering sources started in a easy-going way, because no deadline or target date was set. Then, after the long-term project that finished with the publication of my two-volume work "Gods of the Germanic Peoples", I looked at the TODO list for a small and time-restricted project. That became this one and quickly the project came to life. Rereading the sources and writing started simultaneously and related to this, some contacts flourished with several Facebook friends.

I want to thank **Helga Sagen** for her input, which had led me to some new thoughts which I could process in this treatise. She already had done some similar research herself and offers that at her page at:
http://piereligion.org/easter.html
My thanks also go to colleague author **Carolyn Emerick**, who provided me with some scanned information about Easter lore and customs in English-speaking regions.
http://www.carolynemerick.com/

Lisa Star not only contributed with an excellent proofreading, she also gave quite a few fine proposals for the layout. And **Marada Von Der Manufaktur** pointed me to my many mistakes in the punctuation - I still do not grab the big difference between the comma-rules in German and those in English.
http://de.dawanda.com/shop/Marada

A few other people offered to proofread this book, but due to lack of time and poor health they could not or just for a small part do the job. Nonetheless, grattitude goes to them too for their fine offer.

For any left errors in grammar and spelling or 'strange' verbalizations solely the author is responsible; sometimes he behaves a bit smart-alecky and adds pieces of text after the proofread phase has ended which then are kept unchecked.

Used sources

Illustrations

P. 6: Gods of the Germanic Peoples 2, p. 427.

P. 8: http://special.lib.gla.ac.uk/exhibns/month/jan2001.html

P. 15: https://commons.wikimedia.org/wiki/File:Nuremberg_Chronicle_Venerable_Bede.jpg

P. 16: https://commons.wikimedia.org/wiki/File:S%C3%A9lestat_132,_fol._96v.jpeg

P. 18: http://www.expedition-grimm.de/de/presse/pressefotos.html, © Museum Haldensleben.

P. 19: http://reader.digitale-sammlungen.de/de/fs3/object/display/bsb10435144_00005.html

P. 24: Dahn, Felix und Therese: Walhall. Leipzig, 1903.

P. 27: Historisches Museum Frankfurt. http://commons.wikimedia.org/wiki/File: Karl_der_Grosse_Alte_Bruecke_Frankfurt.jpg

P. 30: Gods of the Germanic Peoples 1, p. 86.

P. 32: http://crossfish.rssing.com/chan-1177470/all_p12.html

P. 37: https://commons.wikimedia.org/wiki/File:Eos.jpg, gemeinfrei.

P. 38: Gods of the Germanic Peoples. From Roman Times to the Viking Age 1, p. 289.

P. 40: http://www.hoefingen.net/suentel/homesue7.htm.

P. 43: http://digitale.bibliothek.uni-halle.de/vd17/content/titleinfo/95650.

P. 44: Smids, Ludolph, Schatkamer der Nederlandsse Oudheden, Amsterdam, 1711.

P. 45: Chaucis, Schildius de, Nobilissimo Veteris Germaniæ Populo Libri Duo, Aurich, 1742.

P. 47: Mushard, Luneberg, De Ostera Saxonum", Bremen, 1700.

P. 48: Hase, Theodor, de saxonum idolo Ostera. In: Bibliotheca historico-philologico-theologica. Classis Octavae Fasciculus Primus, Bremen 1725.

P. 50: Recieved digitally from a citizen of Osterode.

P. 52: Title from the Detroit Publishing Co., catalogue J--foreign section. Detroit, Mich. : Detroit Photographic Company, 1905. Public domain.

P. 54: Baring, Daniel Eberhard, Descriptio Salae, Lemgo, 1744..

P. 55: http://commons.wikimedia.org/wiki/File:Zedler_-_Universal-Lexicon,_Band_1_%28Titelblatt%29.jpg

P. 56: "Braga and Hermode", magazine, volume 3, title page.

P. 56: Braga and Hermode" magazine, volume 3, p. 21.

P. 58: Valvasor, Johann Weichard von, Die Ehre des Herzogthums Crain, Lanbach 1689.

P. 59: https://commons.wikimedia.org/wiki/File:HochsteinFelsen.jpg. Copyright: SchiDD. Vcröffcntlicht unter Creative Commons Attribution-Share Alike 3.0 Unported.

P. 61: https://commons.wikimedia.org/wiki/File:Burgruine_Regenstein_neu.jpg. Copyright: Lencer. Free for any use.

P. 63: Montanus, (Zuccalmaglio, Vincenz Jacob von), Die deutschen Volksfeste, Volksbräuche und deutscher Volksglaube in Sagen, Märlein und Volksliedern. ein Beitrag zur vaterländischen Sittengeschichte, vol. 1, Iserlohn und Elberfeld 1854.

P. 66: https://commons.wikimedia.org/wiki/File:Corvey_Westwerk.png, Picture by Spunky, public domain.

P. 71: Picture by GardenStone, taken at 10.7.2015.

P. 73: König Aldfrith von Northumbria. http://metalarea.org/images/audiocovers/2013_Feb/acov_tid193312.jpg.

P. 76: Stade, Dietrich A. von Historisch-dogmatische Abhandlung von den Fest- Feier- und Sonntagen, Bremen 1795.

P. 76: Simpson, Jacqueline, A piece of Easter lore from "The Folklore of Sussex", London, 1973.

P. 79: http://digital.wlb-stuttgart.de/sammlungen/sammlungsliste/werksansicht/?no_cache=1&tx_dlf[id]=5216&tx_dlf[page]=1.

P. 81: http://commons.wikimedia.org/wiki/File:Easter_Fire.JPG, owner:

ElHeineken, released under the Creative Commons Attribution 3.0 Unported license.

P. 82: Timaeus, Johannes, De Igne Paschali. Von dem Osterfeuwr. (Title shortened), Hamburg, 1590.

P. 87: https://commons.wikimedia.org/wiki/File:Hot_cross_bun.jpg. Copyright: Lausanne Morgan, U.S. Air Force. Public domain.

P. 89: https://commons.wikimedia.org/wiki/File:Ostereier_9.JPG. Copyright: L.Kenzel. Released under the Creative Commons Attribution 3.0 Unported License.

P. 90: Picture GardenStone.

P. 92: Reinsberg-Düringsfeld, Otto Freiherr von, Aberglaube – sitte – Feste Germanischer Völker. Das festliche Jahr, S. 151. In a reprint from the original, Leipzig, 1898.

P. 93: http://www.historicfood.com/Pie%20recipe2.htm.

P. 94: http://www.mopo.de/panorama/ostern-die-zehn-skurrilsten-osterbraeuche-aus-aller-welt,5066860,26876604.html

P. 98: http://commons.wikimedia.org/wiki/File:Osterbrunnen_Mudau_01. JPG, owner: Immanuel Giel. The copyright holder of this work released this work into the public domain.

Literature

Baring, Daniel Eberhard, (Danielis Eberhardi Baringii), Descriptio Salæ principatus Calenbergici locorumque adiacentium Oder Beschreibung der Saala im Amt Lauenstein des Braunschweig-Lüneb. Fürstenthums Calenberg und aller in dieselbe fliessenden Quellen und Bäche, Lemgo 1744.

Bede, The Reckoning of Time, Translated with commentary by Faith Wallis, Liverpool 1999.

Carver, Martin, (Ed.) Sanmark, Alex, (Ed.) Semple, Sarah, (Ed.), Signals of Belief in Early England. Anglo-Saxon Paganism Revisited, Oxford (UK) 2010.

Christian, Roy, Country Life Book of Old English Customs, London 1966.

Clostermeier, Christian Gottlieb, Der Eggesterstein im Fürstenthum Lippe: eine naturhistorische und geschichtliche Monographie, Lemgo 1848.

Dorow, Dr., Die Denkmale germanischer und römischer Zeit in den Rheinisch-Westfälischen Privinzen, Stuttgart und Tübingen 1823.

Einhard, Vita Karoli Magni. Das Leben Karls des Großen, Lateinisch-Deutsch, Übersetzt von Evelyn Scherabon Firchow, Stuttgart 1968–1981.

Ernesti, Johann, Heinrich, Martin, Miscellaneen zu deutschen Alterthumskunde, Geschichte und Statistik, Halle 1794.

Falckenstein, Johann, Heinrichs von, Analecta Nordgaviensia, Schwabach, 1734.

Fiske, John, Myths and Myth-Makers old tales and superstitions, interpreted by comparative mythology, Petersham 1872.

GardenStone, Gods of the Germanic Peoples. From Roman Times to the Viking Age, vol. 1 and 2, Norderstedt 2014.

GardenStone, The Nerthus claim, Norderstedt 2012.

Geißler, Dr. Horst, Repetitorium der deutschen Literaturgeschichte, Weimar 1917.

Gilst, Aat van, Wijze vrouwen en godinnen, Soesterberg 2014.

Grimm, Jacob, Deutsche Mythologie, Bände 1, 2 und 3, Reprint der Ausgabe von 1875–78, Wiesbaden 1992.

Grimm, Jacob, Teutonic Mythology, translated by James Stephen Stallybrass, vol. I - IV, London, 1882 - 1888.

Hase, Theodor, de saxonum idolo Ostera. In: Bibliotheca historico-philologico-theologica. Classis Octavae Fasciculus Primus, Bremen 1725.

Hazlitt, W. Carew, Faith and Folklore of the British Isles, 2 volumes, New York 1965, in a reprint of the 1905 edition.

Hocker, Nikolaus, Deutscher Volksglaube in Sang und Sage, Göttingen 1853.

Klemm, Dr. Gustav Friedrich, Handbuch der Germanischen Alterthümer, Dresden 1836.

Krantz, Albertus, Wandalia, Frankfurt, 1575.

Letzner, Johannes, Historia S. Bonifacij. Der Teutschen Apostel genandt. Hildesheim 1602.

Looijenga, Tineke, The Bergakker Find and its Context. In: Pforzen und Bergakker. In; Neue Untersuchungen zu Runeninschriften, (hg.) Bammesberger, Alfred, S. 145–147, Göttingen 1999.

Meyer, Elard Hugo, Volkskunde. Geschichte der deutschen Lebensweise und Kultur. Reprint from the original from Strassburg 1898.

Montanus, (Zuccalmaglio, Vincenz Jacob von), Die deutschen Volksfeste, Volksbräuche und deutscher Volksglaube in Sagen, Märlein und Volksliedern. ein Beitrag zur vaterländischen Sittengeschichte, vol. 1, Iserlohn und Elberfeld 1854.

Münchhausen, Karl, Freiherrn von, Wold und Ostar, zwei altdeutsche Gottheiten. In: Gräter, F.D., Bragur und Hermode, oder Neues Magazin für die väterländischen Alterthümer, Leipzig 1798.

Mushard, Luneburg, M., De Ostera Saxonum, Bremen 1700.

Page, R.I., Anglo-Saxon Paganism: The Evidence of Bede. In: Pagans and Christians, edited by T. Hofstra and others, pp. 99–129, Groningen 1995.

Pegg, Bob, Rites and Riots. Folk customs of Britain and Europe, Poole 1981.

Perger, Anton von, Deutsche Pflanzensagen, Stuttgart 1864.

Piderit, Johann, Chronicon Comitatus Lippiae, Das ist: Ejgentliche Vnd Auszführliche Bescheibunge Aller Antiquiteten vnd Historien der Vhralten Graffschafft Lipp, Rinteln an der Weeser 1627.

Pollington, Stephen, The Elder Gods. The Otherworld of Early England, Little Downham 2011.

Porter, Enid, Folklore of East Anglia, Batsford 1974.

Pröhle, Heinrich, Harzsagen, Band 1, Leipzig 1859.

Reinsberg-Düringsfeld, Otto Freiherr von, Aberglaube–Sitte–Feste Germanischer Völker. Das festliche Jahr. Reprint der Originalausgabe, Leipzig 1898.

Schaumann, A.F.H., Geschichte des niedersächsischen Volkes, Göttingen 1839.

Schildii De Caucis, Joannis, Nobilissimo Veteris Germaniæ Populo Libri Duo, Aurich Tapper 1742.

Shaw, Philip A., Pagan Goddesses in the Early Germanic World. Eostre, Hreda and the Cult of Matrons, London 2011.

Simpson, Jacqueline, The Folklore of Sussex, Batsford 1973.

Slocum. Jonathan, An Anglo-Saxon Dictionary, University of Texas, Linguistics Research Center in The College of Liberal Arts, Austin 2009.

Smids, Ludolph., M.D., Schatkamer der Nederlandsse Oudheden, Amsterdam 1711.

Stade, Dietrich A. von, Historisch-dogmatische Abhandlung von den Fest- Feier- und Sonntagen, Bremen 1759.

Stübner, Johann Christoph, Merkwürdigkeiten des Harzes überhaupt und des Fürstenthums Blankenburg, Band 1, Halberstadt 1793.

Timaeus, Johannes, De Igne Paschali. Von dem Osterfeuwr. (Title shortened), Hamburg, 1590.

Valvasor, Johann Weichard von, Die Ehre des Herzoglhums Crain, Lanbach 1689.

Vulpius, Christian August, Curiositäten der physisch literarisch artistisch historischen Vor- und Mitwelt, Band 2, S. 458f., Weimar 1812.

Wasserbach, Ernst Casimir, Dissertatio de statua illustri Harminii, Lemgo 1698.

Wilson, David, Anglo-Saxon Paganism, London 1992.

Wolf, J. W., Beiträge zur deutschen Mythologie 1: Götter und Göttinnen, Göttingen – Leipzig 1853.

Zautner, Andreas E., Der gebundene Mondkalender der Germanen, Leipzig 2013.

Zedler, Johann Heinrich, Grosses vollständiges Universal-Lexicon aller Wissenschaften und Künste, vol. 24, p.1114, 2201, Halle und Leipzig 1731–1754.

Webpages

http://www.hoefingen.net/suentel/homesue7.htm

http://www.legendsofeostra.com/meet-eostra-rabbit/

http://www.brauchtumsseiten.de/a-z/o/ostara/home.html

Altenglisches Wörterbuch (Old English Dictionary) http://www.koeblergerhard.de/aewbhinw.html

Der Eggesterstein im Fürstenthum Lippe.pdf http://digital.ub.uni-paderborn.de/download/pdf/1002405?name=Der%20Eggesterstein%20im%20F%C3%BCrstenthum%20Lippe 37 [19] – §. 6.

Von der Verehrung der Göttin Easter oder Eostra am Eggersteine insbesondere. UB Digital–Digitale Sammlungen http://digital.ub.uni-paderborn.de/ihd/content/pageview/1119164

Council of Austerfield – Wikipedia, the free encyclopedia http://en.wikipedia.org/wiki/Council_of_Austerfield

Ostern in Deutschland http://www.german-easter-holiday.com/ostern-osterfest/ostern/

Easter, Eostre, or Ishtar? http://www.jonsorensen.net/2012/04/04/easter-eostre-or-ishtar/

Myths and myth-maker http://stacklife.harvard.edu/item/myths-and-mythmakers/9B9E305F-F069-C241-88EF-35CDAD6973FF

Die Externsteine – ein Aufbewahrungsort für Missetäter ? Heimat Lipperland http://heimat.lippe-owl.de/die-externsteine-ein-aufbewahrungsort-fuer-missetaeter/

Sagen und Geschichten http://www.hoefingen.net/suentel/homesue7.htm

„an dem osterteynen" http://www.lagis-hessen.de/de/subjects/idrec/sn/fln/id/664103

http://www.havausave.de/osterstein.htm

http://digitale.bibliothek.uni-halle.de/id/1000519

http://www.hvv-hoexter.de/wp-content/uploads/2010/08/Das-Blutbad-von-Hoexter.pdf

http://www.catholic.org/encyclopedia/view.php?id=4116

Index

A

Æcerbot 67, 69
Ælfric 14
Æstar 57
Ackermonath 26
Aestorhild 74
Aldfrith of Northumbria 72, 73
Anton Ritter von Perger 65
April 1, 7, 19, 20, 22, 25, 26, 35, 46, 57, 77
Aprilis 11, 26
Arminius 43, 44
Astaroth 57
Astarte 55
Austerfield 72
Austerthal 74
austra 19, 20, 31, 33, 36
Austriahena 1, 29, 30, 31
Austriahenae 23, 29

B

Batavian 39
Bede 4, 7, 11, 13, 16, 17, 18, 19, 22, 26, 46, 48, 57, 77, 85, 97
Belgium 78
Blankenburg 51, 52, 60, 61
Bocksthorn 84
bonfire 57, 81, 82, 83, 84, 85, 86, 91
Boniface 21, 84, 85
Braga and Hermode 56, 102
Brandenburg 50
Bremen 85
British Isles 78
Brocken 49
Brunswick 82

C

Cambridgeshire 74
Carolingian 42
charcoal 91
Charlemagne 25, 26, 27, 60, 96
Chemnitz 53
Cherusci 43
Christian August Vulpius 84
Christian Wilhelm Flügge 97
Christoph Friedrich Fein 51
Cologne 21, 29, 31
Conradus Fontanus of Huxar 84

Corvey 62, 63, 65, 66, 67

D

Daniel Eberhard Baring 53
Denmark 23
De temporum ratione 7
Diana 51
Dietrich A. von Stade 76
Dortmund 82
Dutch 39, 44

E

Easter Bunny 78, 80
Easter eggs 78, 89
Easter Eggs 79, 80
Easter-laughing 91
Easterwine 74
Easterwulf 74
Ēastre 19
Eastrington 74
Eastry 72, 74
egg-game 88
Einhard 4, 25, 104
Elstra 59, 61
Embolismic 11
England 17, 18, 19, 21, 22, 23, 26, 31, 67, 77

Eos 33, 37
Eostar 1, 3, 22, 39, 49, 50, 55, 62, 63, 64, 67
ēoster 72, 74
Eosturmonath 7, 10, 26
Equinox 85
Estrey 72
Externsteine 1, 51, 52

F

fertility 10, 19, 21, 39, 77, 80, 86, 94
fountains 94
France 85
Frankfurt 27
Frankish 21, 25

G

Gambach 70, 71
Georg Franck of Franckenau 80
Germania 75
Germany 5, 10, 21, 22, 23, 40, 46, 48, 49, 51, 74, 78, 80, 82, 85, 97
goat 95
Göttingen 81, 97
Grimm 1, 4, 18, 19, 20, 21, 22, 35

Gustav Klemm 60

H

hare 80, 90, 93
Harz 49, 50, 52, 61, 84
healing powers 94
Heinrich Pröhle 49
Henri the Lion 50
Hesse 70
Hildesheim 82
Hindu 32, 33
Holland 39
Horn 52, 85
Hot cross buns 87
Höxter 62, 65
Hretha 10, 85
hurst 39
Hurstrga 1, 38, 39

J

Jacqueline Simpson 76
Jakob Fürchtegott Dielmann 27
jewelry eggs 89
Johann Christoph Stübner 51, 61
Johannes Gehrt 24
Johannes Letzner 84
Johann Heinrich Martin Ernesti 52

Johann Timaeus 82
Johann Weichard von Valvasor 57
Johann Wilhelm Wolf 70
Jonathan Slocum 34
Jürgen Udolphs 36

K

Karl Georg Friedrich Goes 60
Kent 72
Kohlstädt 43

L

lamb 20, 34, 95
Lestines 83
Lower Saxony 49
Ludolph Smids 44
Luna 57
Luneburg Mushard 46
Lünel 82

M

Mainz 21
Marburg 41
March 7, 20, 22, 25, 26
Mark Ostera 5

Matronae 29, 31
Meinberg 51
Modranecht 9
Montanus 62, 63, 65
Moon 7
Münchhausen 57, 59, 97
Münzenberg 70

N

Nerthus 69
Netherlands 39, 78
Nikolaus Hocker 62
North Rhine-Westphalia 43, 62

O

Ohlenborg 1, 53
Oistirsteynen 1, 70
Oostera 1, 44, 45, 46
Oriental 20, 48
Ostarmanoth 25, 26
ôstarun 21
Osta-Stone 40
Osteralb 46
Osterdorp 48
Osterhagen 48
Osterholt 46
Osterholz 1, 42, 43, 49, 74

Osterode 1, 48, 49, 50, 74
Osterwede 48
Ostirveld 70

P

Paderborn 5
Paschal 10, 13, 20, 26
Paschal lamb 20
Passover 45, 95
Penitentials 14, 16, 17
Phoenicians 57
pigs' bladders 95
Pollyanna Jones 6, 14
pregnant 91
Pustkuchen 51

R

Reinsberg-Düringsfeld 83
Renaissance 96
resurrection 35, 60, 80, 86, 88, 94
Reto 85
Romantic 96

S

Saint Ambrose 80
Saxony-Anhalt 49

Schildius de Chaucis 45, 46

Schlangen 43
Spring 21, 22, 33, 60, 77, 85, 86, 95
Stephen Pollington 13, 14
Sussex 76
Sybil Stone 59
sylvan goddess 53

T

Tacitus 75
Temple 46
Theodorus Hasaeus 48
Thirty Years' War 65
Thuringia 49
Tineke Loojinga 39
torches 88, 91, 95

U

Usha 32, 33

W

Wasserbach 42, 43, 44
Weser Uplands 40
Woden 23

Y

Yorkshire 72, 74

Z

Zedler 1, 5

The New Standard

Gods of the Germanic Peoples

From Roman Times to the Viking Age

This two-volume work offers alphabetic listed information about over 270 deities of the Germanic peoples and covers the time from the Roman Era - the first centuries CE in which the Roman Empire enfolded large parts of the territories of Europe where Germanic peoples lived - up until the Viking Age.

Except for this B/W edition also a beautiful color edition exists with 87 great illustrations in full color; this color edition can ordered from shops in Germany only.

A few random pages can be viewed at:
http://www.chaosowl.net/view-k.pdf

Wild Hunt and Furious Host

Processions of the dead, ghost armies, supernatural hunters, armies from the underworld who pursue or hunt through the sky or on the earth, appear all over the world in very different forms in mythology and folk belief.

This book takes you on a walk through a historical-literary landscape of that popular belief, more specifically the areas where the Wild Hunt, the Wild Hunter and the Furious Host occur.

What makes this book perhaps different from many others, is that there lies a strong emphasis on the multitude of included original sources and texts from the Middle Ages.

Goddess Holle

This book leads through facts, stories, and legends of Frau Holle, often also called Mother Hulda, without any dogmatic prescription and invites the reader to discover the goddess her- or himself and form own opinions.

It will become clear, that Holle is much more than just the figure from the famous fairytale the Grimm brothers published long ago. She can be recognized as an ancient goddess guarding the circle of life of humans from birth to death and beyond.

The book covers various types of information about Frau Holle. Each of nine chapters is devoted to one type of information -- e.g., geographical locations associated with Frau Holle, plant lore, myths from different regions about her, scholarly thoughts on the lore, and at the endeven a small collection of recipes related to Holle.

"The Nerthus claim" is a nonfiction book in which in a rather conversational tone is pointed out how even our most common conceptions about Nerthus may be unfounded. The book contains the results of a research project concerning the goddess Nerthus. We know from this goddess only through Tacitus, who in the first Century CE spoke about her as an earth goddess. In an easy reading way the book discusses the possible meaning of her name, her worshipers, her secret island, her rituals and her possible veneration under other names and in other regions, like e.g. England.

It was about two thousand years ago the Roman historian Tacitus reported the Germanics venerated Mercury above all.
He meant a Germanic God he equated with Mercury. Because Tacitus didn't denominate the name of that God, it had to be interpreted. Many centuries later scholars widely agreed that the name of this God must be Woden. Today that opinion is by many still taken as evidence. This assumption is assayed here on the basis of quite a few available primary sources – the result suggests serious doubts about the entrenched view.